FROM THE RIVER

A guidebook to sobriety from a lifetime
of lessons paddling

Joe Booth

PRAISE FOR FROM THE RIVER

"A soul-searching tome on using lessons learned from the river to see beyond the horizon line of addiction and leave it in your wake. A gratifying and uplifting read for anyone navigating the murky waters of dependence and despair."
Eugene Buchanan, author, Brothers on the Bashkaus, and former editor-in-chief of Paddler magazine

"From the River is a gift from the heart, wisdom, and buoyant spirit of Joe Booth. Joe becomes our river guide through a unique and seemingly effortless blend of neuroscience, psychology, life experiences, recovery wisdom, and adventure writing. His five principles of the Class Five Mind are guideposts for living. Keep a pencil handy because you will find yourself marking many insights and lessons that will speak to you from the pages."
Marya Endriga, Ph.D., Clinical Psychologist

"From The River is such a thought- provoking, clever and honest book. Joe Booth shares his unique approach to life and sobriety with courage, grace and resilience. If you want to live a life of truth and sobriety, this book is a must read!"
Erica Spiegelman, CADAC-II, author, Rewired: A Bold New Approach to Addiction & Recovery

"Athletes and adventurers from all walks of life will identify with the wisdom in From the River. The Class Five Mind principles go far beyond sobriety - they can transform people into the best version of themselves"
Doug Pobst, author, The Heart of Recovery

"It's difficult to find authenticity in this world. It's even more difficult to find it when it leads to vulnerability. Joe's story and struggles were real. But so is the healing power manifested in nature and relationships."
Josh Endres, author, It Was Good: 10 Years in the High Sierra

"Whitewater Kayaking is such a special sport in that it brings out the best in people, and it connects everyone to the environment in such an honest and caring way, a two-way street. Joe is sharing the stories from the perspective of the paddler and for the protection of the river. Nailing a line, keeping your life in balance, or writing a book for others to learn from and enjoy takes effort and commitment. Hats off to Joe for making this book happen for all of us!"
Eric Jackson, World Champion Kayaker and Entrepreneur

"Joe's unique approach to life's challenges and addiction are inspirational. They provide the foundation for the destruction of shame in your life and enhancing a felt sense of well-being. His core principles, proven effective with humility, are an especially powerful tool in developing a healthy community and a healthy sense of self that roots out addiction."
Chip Kern, LCPC

FROM THE RIVER

"Unable to perceive the shape of you, I find you all around me.
Your presence fills my eyes with your love.
It humbles my heart, for you are everywhere."
Hakim Sanai, 11th century Sufi poet

Mesa Falls by Bob Booth

Published on July 4, 2020 by Class Five Mind Inc
Berkeley, California
www.classfivemind.com

Copyright © Joe Booth 2020

Printed and bound in the United States of America

ISBN 978-0-578-67778-1

Editor: Eugene Buchanan
Cover Art: Ben McKenzie
Cover Layout and Internal Design: Josh Endres
Layout Production: Rob Peters

Photography Contributors:

Bob Booth	Travis Lehman
Matt Mounsey	Kenya Otto
Zach Dewell	Scott Springer
Kevin Kennedy	Andrew Daigh
Gregory Lee	Nick Gottlieb
Mareike Delley	Forest Ledger
Dave Steindorf	Pat Rogers
Wes Schrecongost	Team River Runner
William Freihofer	First Descents
Ford Smith	

Proceeds of this book are donated to American Whitewater, First
Descent, and Team River Runner

FROM THE RIVER

A guidebook to sobriety from a lifetime
of lessons paddling

Joe Booth

CLASS FIVE MIND

Class Five Mind, Inc.

TO MY MOM, DAD, AND BROTHER, *who put me on a raft when I was three-years-old and sent me downstream toward a life of adventure and education.*

TO MY WIFE, BRIT, *who saved my life with her courage and love, and continues to inspire me with her resilience and humor.*

CLASS
FIVE
MIND

FOREWORD

"Standing water grows stale."

— **Bruce Lee**

"MY NAME IS JOE, AND I'M AN ALCOHOLIC." I always hated the sound of that. Saying those words made me feel like I was a broken person, stuck as "an alcoholic" forever. That type of identity didn't work for me. I needed to move beyond addiction, not get comfortable with it. I had to put the past behind me and ditch the booze, drugs, thoughts, and habits that landed me with the label in the first place.

Despite what my friends in AA were telling me, I wasn't alone in my objection to carrying a stigma for the rest of my life. The old way of thinking about addiction is changing, and people are beginning to rethink the labels of "alcoholic" and "addict." The notion that we are stuck a certain way for the rest of our lives is unacceptable for this new generation of people in recovery. Many experts now agree that addiction can be conquered with the right combination of mindset, tools, and support.

You and I are adventurous people. We're driven to progress beyond the horizon in search of something new.

I had to know what lay beyond the horizon of addiction. If you're reading this, I have a feeling that you may also want to know what more is out there for you to discover.

We aren't alone. Like a river during spring runoff, sobriety continues to rise in popularity as more celebrities, athletes, and social influencers open up about their decisions to stop drinking or using drugs. Discussions about abstinence are extending beyond the church basements of 12 Step programs into our social media feeds and becoming mainstream. Google keyword searches, such as "how to stop drinking" and "how to get sober," have nearly tripled in popularity over the past 15 years. And if Google says it's true, well, no one can argue with that — not even Bing.

As awareness of sobriety's benefits continues to grow and become more socially accepted, people are searching for other like-minded individuals and resources with which they can identify. That's where *From the River* comes in. This book is my way of contributing to the community I love — my tribe of adventure athletes, weekend warriors, and young adults who get caught in a cycle of being stuck, self-doubt, striving to succeed, and fun at all costs. People like you and I who live to go big but let our guard down and got caught up in a destructive lifestyle.

While there have been numerous books written about recovery, very few speak directly to the heart and soul of the outdoorsman. I hope that nature-lovers seeking inspiration and practical guidance on how to win their battles against substance abuse will appreciate the honesty, metaphors, and advice included in this guidebook for sobriety.

It is a guidebook, indeed. When I began to write it, it was initially intended to be a series of short stories about the lessons I've learned from a lifetime spent on the river, accompanied by guidebook-like descriptions of the trips. Many of the stories in Section II still reflect this original intent — all the way down to logistic details for the reader who wants to experience these exciting sections of whitewater first hand.

But as I typed the stories onto the screen, I gradually realized that many of the lessons I'd taken from the river had also been applied to my recovery. And thus, the Class Five Mind was born — Courage, Commitment, Humility, Resilience, Flow. All traits that apply to running the river as well as the road to sobriety.

An honest reflection into the world of whitewater kayaking, addiction, and transformation, From the River is broken up into two sections — "Section I: Class Five Mind" and "Section II: From the River." In Section I, I call upon my background in psychology, education, and my personal struggle with substance abuse. In this section, I offer science-based, practical advice on how to break the chains of addiction by developing a mindset that every adventure athlete and weekend warrior can relate to. In Section II, I share lessons and anecdotes that I learned from my years paddling with cancer survivors and blind veterans. This section also contains detailed and thrilling accounts of overcoming the mental and physical challenges of paddling Class V whitewater.

Although it began as a guidebook, the final intention of this book is to act as a resource and motivation to help you along your own journey to sobriety.

No one can get sober, or master the nuances of running

whitewater, by merely reading a book. Addiction is an insidious condition that is extremely complex and difficult to beat. Social, physical, spiritual, and psychological factors all come into play when dealing with addiction. *From the River* should be used in combination with other resources to help you sufficiently build new habits and move into recovery. While the psychological theories and neurological processes discussed in this book are grossly oversimplified for brevity's sake, their relevance is sound — our brains are powerfully equipped with all of the necessary hardware and software to help change our lives.

For most of us who have struggled with addiction, we know that it can be a dark, lonely place. If you are living in that sad, empty place right now — please hear these words — your life will get better if you're willing to put in the work and get sober. There's a rainbow waiting for you on

> **Google keyword searches, such as "how to stop drinking" and "how to get sober," have nearly tripled in popularity over the past 15 years.**

the other side of the waterfall's horizon. But if you want to see that rainbow, you have to be willing to get in your boat and paddle through the fear that's been holding you back.

If you're self-medicating to numb your depression, anxiety, or any other mental health issue, use the local resources available to you. A quick Google search will point you to therapists and support groups that can help. If you're suicidal, put down this book and call an expert right now. Regardless of your struggle — you deserve a good life, no matter what you've been told or think about yourself. One of the biggest lessons I learned from my recovery is that I have to be humble and brave enough to ask for help. There are people out there who can help you through this. They can help you paddle your boat. I've experienced it myself — people I barely knew, and others I assumed had written me off, were willing to jump in the raft and help me navigate beyond the horizon of addiction.

You don't have to go it alone. The river is wide enough for all who wish to paddle in its waters. I hope these lessons from the river help you along your voyage.

See you downstream!

INTRODUCTION
Class Five Mind

Solo mission on the Gallatin by Joe Booth

AT THE AGE OF 36, I found myself in a 40-day addiction rehab center. I was emotionally and financially wrecked and on the verge of divorce. Broken and confused, I contemplated how someone like me could end up in a place like this. I had always viewed myself as a winner — first in my family to graduate from college, Eagle Scout, accomplished outdoorsman, budding career in the tech industry. I didn't think rehab and bankruptcy were for people like me.

But I was wrong. I was there, surrounded by other addicts wondering how they ended up there, too — men like me, who had avoided facing their problems and never learned how to live life on life's terms. People who had also excelled in a variety of areas but whose lives were entirely out of balance. Other guys who tried to escape reality, just like I had.

As I reflected upon my circumstances, many questions raced through my mind: What happened to the boy that just wanted to play in the mountains? What sort of man did I want to be? How could I allow my actions to hurt my loved ones? How could I rebuild the damaged relationships? What was the lesson of all this? How could I turn my life around? Could I use this experience to help people?

With the help and guidance of others, I began an inner journey of self-discovery which provided deep insights into my shortcomings along with answers to many of the questions I faced. This process of deep self-reflection, brutal honesty, and accountability revealed parts of myself that I didn't realize were there. One of these was an emotional side that had been neglected for as long as I could remember.

In our culture, boys are raised to suppress their emotions. Anger and happiness are the only two that are socially acceptable. The former being unwelcome, but tolerated; and the latter being used as a justification for any behavior that "makes you happy." As boys, we don't learn to feel the broad range of emotions that are part of the human experience. Instead, we have to balance the line of anger or happiness, aloof to other emotions that make up 90 percent of our day. So what do people do? We seek out happiness at all costs and get angry when we don't find it. Why? It's all we have been taught to do since we were kids. The problem is that as little boys turn into young men this imbalance can have negative effects on areas of our lives that rely on us to be responsible, mature and considerate. Throw in a little thrill-seeking, selfishness, drugs and alcohol, and you have a recipe for personal disaster. That's exactly what happened to me.

Like many adventure-seeking young adults, when I was in my mid-20s I was the epitome of living the so-called "dream." Residing in a small mountain town in Montana, I would snowboard all winter, kayak the rest of the year, while partying the entire time. It was an adrenaline-fueled lifestyle centered on "going big" and having fun. For years, I felt like I was indestructible. Life was fast-paced, simple, and loaded with excitement. But it was a selfish, ego-driven lifestyle that left me feeling empty.

No matter how much I had accomplished on the river or mountain, there was always a need to prove myself on bigger and more challenging runs. Even when I found myself in exotic locations running picturesque drops, I still felt "less than." There was a hole inside me that I tried to fill with excitement, adventure, and fun. When that didn't work, I turned to drugs and alcohol.

I was trapped in an unspoken cycle that affects many people in our community. Yes, whitewater kayaking, like many other adventure sports, has a dark side. Not the lightsaber battle, "Luke, I am your father" dark side. But an undeniable blight which is rarely discussed openly, despite its effect on so many folks.

That's right, kayaking isn't all fist bumps and paddling crystal clear water. For some, the drive to go bigger and bigger can leave them feeling emotionally empty. The coming and going of seasonal adventure buddies can leave a person wondering who their real friends are and left feeling lonely and isolated. Beers at the take-out can lead to drinking and driving back home. Smoking pot at the put-in can become a routine warm-up exercise to "get your head right." Sound like anyone you know? Eventually for some, the kayaking and partying go hand-in-hand and they find themselves in this pleasure-seeking cycle: Go big, feel drained, drink or smoke a chemical pick-me-up, go big, feel drained, drink or smoke a chemical pick-me-up, rinse and repeat.

There's another vicious cycle that paddlers like myself can also fall into. It may not be as destructive to the liver or lungs as the drinking and smoking outlined above, but it can be just as emotionally damaging. It's the cycle of taking your adventure way too seriously. An obsession of training so intensely and focusing myopically on improving your paddling that other areas of your life suffer. My accomplishments on the river gave me a sense of pride and freedom that I wasn't getting in other areas in my life. But off the river, my life was falling apart. Relationships can suffer. It's almost cliché to hear paddlers complain about how their significant others don't understand why they kayak so much. Careers can suffer or never materialize. Despite their best intentions, some paddlers have trouble breaking out of the seasonal job-hopping or part-time gigs they became accustomed to in their early river-chasing years. Finances can suffer. Kayaking gear and gas money add up quick when you drive to the river all the time and don't have a steady job to pay the bills. While these may not seem like a big deal when you're "living the dream," routinely neglecting these important areas of my life eventually caught up to me and left me feeling like a loser.

Possibly worst of all, the saddest fate for a kayaker is when the love of paddling fades away. Even though I treasure kayaking and took it very seriously, eventually I lost the enjoyment I once had for it. Instead, I would use kayaking as a form of escapism, pushing off the bank and leaving the world behind. My weeknights became compulsive training sessions on the local Class IV run, practicing methodically to prepare for the weekend's Class V adventure. Weekend trips became missions to run more and more intense whitewater. If I failed in any way — a swim, a portage — I would beat myself up, and the trip would be a waste. The joy I once found on the river was gone, replaced with self-deprecation and unattainable expectations.

The pressure I put on myself to succeed on the river quickly became overshadowed by the reality of my lack of

> **The joy I once found on the river was gone, replaced with self-deprecation and unattainable expectations.**

success in the real world. Despite my repeated attempts to avoid adult responsibility, the dam eventually broke, and I found myself being swept away. My preferred coping methods of avoidance and addiction were failing me. I was struggling with money and relationships, and would soon hit financial rock bottom: my car was repossessed, our condo was foreclosed on, and I made the dreadful decision to file for bankruptcy. The horrific death of my mom and other family traumas threw me even deeper into depression and anxiety. My downward spiral continued as my struggle with addiction threatened my marriage, job, and relationships with my family.

After leaving rehab, I took the next year off from kayaking and snowboarding to focus on the most essential things in my life: my wife, my family, a spiritual foundation, and my job. I began developing a set of principles that would allow me to find joy and contentment again. Because river water runs through my veins, I based this new personal ethos on lessons I learned from the river. The *Class Five Mind* was born. It consists of five basic principles: Courage, Commitment, Humility, Resilience, and Flow!

Courage: Apply the courage developed from facing unknown obstacles in adventure sports to other challenges in personal and professional life.

Commitment: Just like you would commit to a line in a rapid, follow through on the promises made to friends, family, coworkers, and yourself.

Humility: Use the humility learned from portaging rapids to recognize your limitations, work on those areas, learn from others, and accept your help.

Resilience: The resilience of getting back in your boat after a swim teaches you that some failures in life can be overcome by perseverance.

Flow: The precious flow of being wholly present and connected to nature shows that you can also find rhythm, purpose, and mindfulness in other aspects of life.

Simply put, life is like a Class V river.

So why call this set of principles the *Class Five Mind*? Simply put, life is like a Class V river. Like paddling big water, to succeed in life, a certain mindset must be cultivated and maintained. Whether it's long and challenging or short and intense, life is filled with obstacles and violent rapids which expose a person to risk, but also present opportunities. There will be moments of terror and joy, excitement and calm, risk and reward. Sometimes you need to eddy-out to catch your breath. Other times you must focus and paddle as hard as you can. There will be times when you get bumped off your line and must fight to get back on track. Seasons when you swim and seasons when you lace every line. There will be moments of crisis when you'll need someone to throw you a rope. And, some times, others will rely on you for help. On the river, as in life, we move from one wave to the next trying to remain present, but always planning one move ahead, with past experiences swirling in the back of our minds. The river does not care if we live or drown, just as life does not care if we fail or succeed. However impartial the river may be, it always offers guidance on safe passage for those willing to study carefully. The "line" may not always be visible but it's always there.

As the years go by, I work continuously on applying a *Class Five Mind* to all the critical things in my life. By doing so, I have found balance and contentment beyond what I could have ever thought possible when I was "living the dream" in my 20s. Just as improving my paddling skills made me a better kayaker on the river, the mental skills I've developed have also helped me navigate some of the most difficult obstacles of life off the water. I've been able to overcome addiction, trauma, financial hardship, and relationship issues. I used to live in the shadows of shame and guilt. Now I'm proud of the person I have become. I'm proud to say that I have remained sober. My amazing, beautiful wife and I are closer than we have ever been. I have a solid career which has helped me earn financial stability and self-respect. By applying the lessons I learned on the river to other areas of my life, I've been able to transform from being a struggling dirtbag into a responsible and happy adult. This was no easy task for a guy like me, nor is it for many individuals caught in a destructive cycle of pushing limits, self-doubt, and fun at all costs.

I am not the greatest kayaker ever, nor even the best boater I know. To quote kayaking author and cartoonist William Nealy, "I'm just an average boater who gets scared and swims and occasionally wrecks a boat." But the river taught me to get back in the boat and continue to paddle. And to do so with courage, commitment, humility, resilience and flow. Without that lesson, I don't know where I would be today. I'd probably be another lonely aging dirtbag searching for the next adventure, desperate for fleeting camaraderie, caught in a cycle of happiness and anger.

Although it took hitting rock-bottom, I feel very fortunate that my voyage of self-discovery brought me back to nature and the lessons it teaches. This connection to the river of life is the *Class Five Mind*. When developed and applied, it can provide you with success both on and off the river. Just like kayaking, the more you practice these principles, the easier they are to apply when you need them, and the greater the reward downstream. Adventure athletes are talented individuals in their pursuits for challenge and accomplishment. Why not leverage that personality trait into something bigger than another weekend trip? Next time you step out of the woods and make the drive home, take the skills that you've developed in the mountains with you. Pause a moment to visualize everything you can accomplish if you live your everyday life with such passion. You'd be unstoppable!

CHAPTER 01

COMMITMENT

"Do or do not, there is no try."

— Master Yoda

Matt Mounsey in The Pinch by Zach Dewell

SITTING IN A CALM EDDY above a difficult rapid can be a lonely place of contemplation. It's in the safety of this pool that the decision must be made to paddle or portage. You're the only one who can determine whether or not you successfully navigate the water. Even if you've scouted the rapid with the help of your fellow boaters, watched as other kayakers made it down with style, and you have friends in safety positions along the river's banks — for a moment it's just you and the river. The result depends on your willingness to put in the effort necessary to succeed. Even with all of the preparation and excitement of running the rapid, you're not fully committed until you've crossed the boiling eddy-line separating the calm pool from the swift and powerful current.

The eddy-line represents the barrier which divides those who are willing to follow through with their plans and the others who sit and dream about goals they aren't willing to work toward. There's no turning back once you cross that line; you either navigate the water or suffer the consequences of failure.

—Excerpt from the chapter "We Are All Between Swims: Tobin, North Fork Feather River" on page 74

I used to hate myself for living a selfish and reckless lifestyle. My downward spiral affected every aspect of my life and the lives of others. Although I desperately wanted to get off the destructive path that I was on, I wasn't able to. I would get sucked back in by my lack of self-control and entitlement. For years I tried to sober up, be a better husband, and come to terms with where life had taken me. But despite my desire to change, I couldn't commit to the new life I desperately needed.

There was one thing that I was able to commit to, though: kayaking. I've felt a deep connection to rivers since I was a kid, so it was easy to dedicate myself to this self-indulgent activity focused on fun and adventure. For years, kayaking was my number one priority. Each spring, I would set specific goals of the types of skills I wanted to learn or river expeditions to accomplish. These were usually short-term goals filled with adrenaline-rushed milestones to satisfy my ego and the pressure I put on myself to succeed. And guess what? I got really good. Over the years, I put in a ton of miles on the river, surrounded myself with great paddlers, and practiced like crazy. Some days were super fun, others frustrating and scary. The river held me accountable for every paddle stroke and let me know if I was ready to move on to more difficult water or not. Eventually, I was sending waterfalls, charging steep creeks, and navigating big water. It took hard work, practice, and scary swims, but I became a solid paddler.

Unfortunately, the joy and success I experienced on the river was a stark contrast to my life off the water. On the river, I felt a sense of control in the chaos, sure of my strokes, and thought that my mistakes only affected me. Off the river, I was lost in the chaos, unsure of what to do with myself, and my mistakes affected my loved ones. If I were going to turn my life around, I would have to apply the same strategy I used to become a solid kayaker — I'd have to commit. Maybe I could sober up, be a great husband, have a successful career, and be the type of son my mom would have been proud of. So I decided to apply the lessons I learned on the river about commitment to other areas of my life. I set goals, practiced skills, developed new habits, surrounded myself with positive people, and made myself accountable for my actions.

Why is it so hard for some people to commit? That can be a difficult question to answer. But it usually comes down to just a few simple reasons: Our brains don't want to change, there's a lack of motivation, or we simply don't know how to commit. The good news is that for each of these barriers, there's a practical way to overcome them. It can be done the same way a kayaker would study a rapid to find safe passage. First, we need to decide on a destination. Then identify the obstacles we may encounter along the way. Once we have our plan in place, it's up to us to get in our boat, paddle across the eddy-line, and commit to the current.

The first obstacle to commitment is our own brain. That's right. A fantastic three-pound glob of fat and water, we call a brain, is holding us back. Why? Through evolution (if you believe in that sort of thing) the brain developed two fundamental rules, which it obeys in strict order: #1 stay alive, and #2 conserve energy. One way our brain saves energy is by sticking to routines. The brain finds comfort in predictive patterns because it knows what to expect and exactly how much energy will be needed to complete the sequence. This equilibrium forms our daily routines and lifestyles. Unfortunately, our brain doesn't only hold onto patterns that benefit us. When we've developed unhealthy habits, our mind perpetuates those, too. These can come in harmful forms like addiction and negative self-talk, or minor things like scrolling mindlessly through social media. As complicated as these types of behaviors may be, they're still just deeply

The brain developed two fundamental rules: Stay Alive and Conserve Energy.

rooted habits which can be broken. If we want to stop one negative practice, we need to replace it with something positive. Out with the old and in with the new! The brain loves predictive patterns. A trick to changing any habit is to develop new routines, a new default mode for our brain that benefits you.

In order to commit to a major life change, there has to be significant motivation. Which usually comes in the forms of Reward (gain something) and Consequence (lose something). My motivation for sobering-up came in both types. I hoped that I might one day be able to sleep at night, free of guilt and shame — a simple reward for a significant commitment. I had the desire to make it happen, but no matter how bad I wanted to change, I wasn't able to. Eventually, my marriage and career began falling apart due to my addictions. At which point, my wife told me that if I didn't get my shit together, she would leave my dirtbag ass. It wasn't until I was faced with immediate consequences that I was willing to do whatever it took to change my ways. So I took every step possible and sought out help from various resources. I was clueless about the steps to recovery, but I was motivated to take action to avoid the consequences.

These types of situations happen in life all the time. Most people have a desire to change or improve something

> ## Little actions, practiced consistently, will lead to big results.

about themselves. They know the rewards might be significant. But sometimes it's not until we're faced with the consequences of losing something we value, that we are willing to take action. This peculiar behavior is known as "Loss Aversion." It theorizes that people prefer avoiding losses more than acquiring equivalent gains. Which means that if there are consequences, we are more likely to follow through on commitments than if there are only rewards. That's why accountability, by someone other than yourself, is such a strong motivator.

Just like when we are on the river and there is a risk of drowning if we don't give 100 percent, when we are held accountable for our actions, we're more likely to act. The concept of loss aversion aligns neatly with the brain's desire to remain in equilibrium — when life as we know it is threatened, following through on commitments is more likely. Our brains are ready to rise to the challenge when we need them. And when there are significant consequences to our actions, we're much more likely to put in the effort to avoid those consequences. Or in my case, my wife telling me that if I didn't get my shit together, she would leave me. I didn't want to lose her, so I was willing to do whatever I needed to straighten up. Without that consequence, I don't know if I would have been able to find sobriety, and my life would have continued its downward spiral. I needed to be held accountable by someone other than myself.

But even with all of the desire and motivation to change, some people still don't know how to commit. That's when practical steps need to be followed. This is when we talk about building healthy new habits to replace the destructive old ones. Here are a few tactics you can use to begin to follow through on commitments:

FIND ROLE MODELS: If you want to soar with eagles, don't cluck around with chickens. The people we spend the most time with will have the most influence on our lives, our perception, and our long term goals. Seek out groups of people who have already accomplished what you're working toward. Learn from their mistakes and use their success as motivation. Be humble and allow yourself to try new methods that may seem counterintuitive. Just like you would seek out "better kayakers" to paddle with when you were new to the sport, surround yourself with people who can help you reach your goals of a better life.

BUILD MOMENTUM: Little actions, practiced consistently, will lead to big results. Following through with a commitment builds self-confidence. As you change the way you see yourself, eventually you'll begin to believe that you are the type of person capable of accomplishing whatever you put your mind to. The momentum you build by reaching one goal will lead to the next. Soon, your new modus operandi will be one of follow-through and execution. Just like you need to paddle hard to build momentum so you can blast through a big rapid, use the energy you create with each small accomplishment to propel you toward your big goal.

ELIMINATE DISTRACTIONS: Staying focused on a goal is a lot easier if you remove some of the obstacles that hold you back. Get rid of the people, activities, or objects that interfere with your personal goals. Telling a friend "no" when they ask you to go party might seem awkward at first. But real friends will be supportive if you take a brief moment to explain your priorities. If they don't understand, ditch that loser. If you're not working toward your own goals, then you will be working for someone else's. Our modern world is filled with so many distractions. It's up to you to evaluate what's contributing to your success and what's keeping you stuck. Prioritize what's essential and control the environment around you. Just like in a kayak, stay focused on paddling a clean line by avoiding the hazards in your path.

Commitment is one of the strongest attributes of successful people and builds self-confidence. While paddling across a surging eddy-line into a ripping current is exhilarating, it takes practice to learn. So does the ability to stay focused on a goal and eliminate distractions consistently. But commitment isn't about willpower. It's about building an entirely new default setting. Understanding the two highest faculties of the brain (stay alive and conserve energy) provides some insight into why it's so hard to follow through with commitments and how we can overcome bad habits. Since the brain finds comfort in predictive patterns, we need to override the old operating system by developing new habits. Eventually, the new daily rituals become our brain's new default. Building habits and routines that support your goal will build confidence and momentum. But sometimes our internal motivation isn't strong enough. That's when we need role models and accountability partners to help nudge us back onto the right path. As you stick to this new way of behaving, you'll find you're more comfortable and relaxed crossing that eddy-line and commiting to your goals downstream.

CHAPTER 02

COURAGE

"Courage is resistance to fear, mastery of fear, not absence of fear."

— Mark Twain

Dave Schroeder in Quake by Kevin Kennedy

21

AS THE WALL of whitewater consumed AJ, his story flashed in front of my eyes: being ambushed by enemy forces, frantically trying to save his fellow soldiers, the explosion that robbed him of sight, months lying on a hospital bed, a decade of self-medicating to cope with PTSD, the doctors pleading with him to change his life or die alone in his house, and the courage he summoned to survive. Humbled by what I was witnessing, I thought of my own struggles with addiction and the strength it took to get sober. My transformation paled in comparison to what AJ has gone through.

Despite what his "Blind Kayaker" orange vest labeled him, when we came out the other side of Boat Eater, he was a different man in my eyes.

At that moment, AJ wasn't a blind kayaker. He wasn't a blind athlete anymore. He was no longer a wounded vet. Plain and simple, when AJ dropped into that hole and blasted out the other side, he was transformed into one thing and one thing only: a kayaker.

—Excerpt from the chapter "Outtasight: Yankee Jim Canyon, Yellowstone River" on page 98

Courage comes in many forms. It can be seen as a strength in the face of pain, or as the ability to take action despite fear. In the case of kayaking, courage can most obviously be associated with running a significant rapid at the risk of injury or death. But there are other aspects of kayaking that take courage too — like deciding to portage a rapid or getting back in your boat after a bad swim. In the "real world" courage is just as important as on the river. We need to overcome our fears about changing careers, developing new relationships, going back to school, sobering up, or improving any aspect of ourselves that we aren't proud of. All these examples require us to be brave while taking on terrifying and difficult challenges.

To paraphrase Mark Twain, courage is not the absence of fear, it's the mastery of it. Fear can be an awareness of imminent danger, perceived risk, or the memory of failed past experiences. But despite its bad reputation, fear is a vital emotion too often neglected and condemned in society, especially among males. Fear keeps us out of trouble and helps us stay alive. Without it, humans would have never evolved to where we are today. Recognition and control of fear are critical for presence of mind and understanding risk. Most importantly, without it we wouldn't feel the sense of accomplishment that comes with achievement. Courage wouldn't have meaning if not for fear. But if we can't overcome fear, it can hold us back.

Since fear is so condemned in our culture, it's helpful to understand what it is and what it isn't. To start, it's important to distinguish between fear and excitement, which often present themselves simultaneously when a threat is detected. Since excitement and fear both start with our body's sympathetic nervous system (which triggers our Fight, Flight or Freeze response), understanding the similarities and differences between the *physical* state of excitement and the *psychological* state of fear is useful.

A short lesson in neurology provides some insight. Our amygdala is a little olive-sized organ deep in the center of our brain. When a threat is perceived (scary rapid, mean boss, dark alley, debt collector), the amygdala immediately triggers a chain reaction of stress hormones into our bloodstream. This hormonal cocktail includes adrenaline and cortisol. Adrenaline hits us almost instantly, causing increased heart rate, rapid breathing, muscle constriction, and dilated pupils. Most adventure athletes have a love affair with adrenaline. Cortisol, however, is released slowly, over minutes, rather than seconds. It redirects blood to our extremities, away from our digestive tract, and helps maintain the body's focus until the threat has passed. Ever get butterflies in your stomach before doing something intimidating? That's cortisol at work. Adrenaline pumps you up and provides a feeling of excitement. Cortisol enables you to focus on the task at hand. So depending on the person and situation, this mix of hormones results in some type of action: We take on the challenge (Fight), we run away (Flight), or we lock up (Freeze).

What's all this hormonal talk have to do with courage? Let's put it into kayaking terms: Stepping up and running a big drop (Fight). Portaging a rapid (Flight). Scouting a rapid for an absurdly long time, unable to make a decision (Freeze). Now let's put it into a real-life scenario: Your boss is pissed off and walking toward you. You can: A. Punch him in the face, immediately followed by a touchdown dance (Fight), B. Run and hide in the bathroom while scrolling Instagram (Flight), or C. Stand against the wall and pretend you're a lamp (Freeze). Any of these scenarios would be acceptable given the circumstances of being scared of your angry boss and blaming your reaction on hormones.

The timing and roles of adrenaline and cortisol relate back to the physical state of excitement and the psychological state of fear. Simply put, excitement is the body's *physical* response to a stimulus (rapid heart rate). Fear is the *belief* that something terrible is going to happen (scared of a perceived result). Adrenaline helps our body rise to the challenge immediately (excitement), while cortisol sustains our awareness of a threat until it has passed (fear). Fear and excitement aren't the same things, but they often come on at the same time. Which is good because the body's physical excitement is a sign that you're ready to take on a psychological fear. Don't mistake excitement for fear. Use excitement to overcome fear.

We can't stop our body's sympathetic nervous system from trying to keep us out of harm's way. However, we can use techniques to maintain our body's level of excitement without allowing fear to consume us. For example, if we recognize our adrenaline response of an increased heartbeat as preparing our body to take on a physical challenge, we can channel this into a heightened level of awareness to help us make decisions toward our desired outcome. Next time you find yourself in a challenging, scary situation, feel your heartbeat and know that's your body telling you that it's prepared to get out there and crush it! Same thing if you're getting ready for an important meeting or job interview. Excitement means you're ready.

Because cortisol is linked to lingering on a threat, we're more likely to be focused on the potential adverse outcomes as opposed to positive ones. It's also why we tend to analyze things over and over when we get scared. Our body is merely trying to protect itself from the perceived threat. However, if we recognize that it's cortisol causing us to dwell on hazards, we should be able to counteract the negative thoughts by using techniques to reframe the scenario and take action.

So how do we put Mark Twain's words into action — to master fear and act courageously? Now that you're armed with a lesson in kayaker neuroscience, the three tactics below have helped me make it through tough times on and off the water.

> **Instead of focusing on the monster hole, imagine how awesome it will feel to soar over it.**

VISUALIZATION: The brain can't tell the difference between running a rapid in our mind versus actually doing it in our boat. Visualizing yourself running a drop successfully and celebrating at the bottom tricks your brain into thinking that it's already done the job. Which means you can get multiple laps in on a rapid before you've even gotten into your boat. With every successful run visualized, you reduce your anxiety. You can also focus on the positive aspects of a rapid rather than just the hazards. Instead of focusing on the monster hole, imagine how awesome it will feel to soar over it. Use this technique when preparing for challenges off the river, too. Visualize your optimal outcome over and over as you prepare for any task. See yourself living a sober life.

AFFIRMATION: The brain loves positive reinforcement. Affirming yourself in moments of doubt is a great way to build up your confidence quickly. Make a conscious effort to recall positive memories or affirmations that relate specifically to the challenge you are trying to overcome. For example, when sitting in the eddy above an intimidating rapid, I often think of all the different ways I've prepared: I've scouted the line, I've visualized it, I've run similar drops before, my safety is in place, my blood is pumping to my muscles, and I've been kayaking since I was a kid. Doing this mental exercise shifts my mind away from the threat and back toward the goal, which reduces my cortisol levels and the associated fear. In the real world, I often do affirmations when I'm having self-doubt at work, or in my relationships when I am worried about screwing something up. Sounds dorky, but it helps. The assertions remind me that I have what it takes to make good decisions, and as a result, I move forward with confidence. Remind yourself that you have what it takes to live a clean and sober life.

RITUAL: Our brain likes repetition and can be easily fooled. Luckily, we can use these natural tendencies to our advantage by applying a routine to help us calm our minds and bodies. Rituals take our brain out of an energy-zapping problem-solving state of chaos, into a familiar zone where it feels comfortable and safe. Here's a paddling routine that helps me: Regardless of the difficulty of a river or rapid, the first thing I do every time I get in my boat is adjust my seat, then pull on my skirt. Next, I shut my eyes and take a few deep slow breaths, followed by a twist to my right as I reach for my drain plug with my right hand. Then, I twist, reach, and breath to the left. Next, I feel the water with my right, then left hand. I give a few gratitudes to the river, visualize what's ahead, affirm myself, then drop in. While it might sound elaborate, the entire ritual only takes a few seconds. It helps loosen me up physically and connect with the river spiritually. Because I do this every time I get in my boat, not just before a scary rapid, my brain associates the ritual with a familiar, safe and comfortable state. Applying little routines to other parts of the day can be helpful for maintaining a calm mind in any stressful situation. Cut the negative rituals related to your addiction out of your life and replace them with small, but meaningful healthy ones.

By understanding our body and mind connection, we're able to use techniques like this to overcome fear and act in the face of danger. In other words, to be courageous. The more these are practiced, the easier it is to slide back into a calm and brave state of mind. As we overcome more and more scary obstacles, our threshold for fear will grow.

Just don't mistake your body's natural physical state of excitement for the mind's psychological state of fear. Excitement is the desired response to any challenge and is your ally. While fear can be paralyzing, it can be overcome by using techniques like visualization, affirmation, and rituals. Apply this concept toward difficult and frightening obstacles off the river just as you would in your boat.

CHAPTER 03

HUMILITY

"When we have a wider perspective, we have a natural understanding of our place in the great sweep of all that was, is, and will be. This naturally leads to humility and recognition that as human beings we can't solve everything or control all aspects of life. We need others."

— **Douglas Abram,** *The Book of Joy*

Scott Springer in the Kootenai by Bob Booth

EMOTIONS SWEPT over me, and I began to whimper in the eddy as tears of relief and joy flooded my eyes. I could breathe. I was alive. I had made it out. Once my crew arrived and helped me out of the river, I was able to assess my physical state. My fingernails were bleeding from clawing at the rocks in the first eddy I tried to catch. From the face-first collision I had with the river bed, three of my front teeth had been broken into pieces, my chin bled from a deep laceration, and my jaw felt like it was broken. Both of my legs were bruised and bleeding from being dragged over rocks. My right knee felt as if I had torn ligaments and tendons during the foot entrapment. As I lay broken in the eddy, none of the physical pain and injury mattered to me. I was alive. Somehow, I managed to survive.

—*Excerpt from the chapter "Lucky to be Alive: Quake Lake, Madison River" on page 108*

The power and beauty of the river can humble even the most seasoned and prideful paddler. Despite your ability on the water, there will always be rapids that you can't handle. Regardless of how many rainbows you've seen in the sky, you will still be left in awe by those hiding in waterfall grottos. It's in those captivating moments that we're reminded of the majesty of the river and our place among it. Anyone who has ever been swept away by rushing water has felt its unyielding weight. It's the same force that carves the Grand Canyon and reshapes shorelines every spring. As kayakers, we're made aware of this power every time we paddle our boats. And the sport is humbling in many ways. It's an adventure in letting go, accepting our limitations, and connecting with others.

Like many activities in life, kayaking is a balancing act of self-confidence and reserve. A constant tension exists between pushing ourselves and just going with the flow. Moments when we need to paddle beyond our fear and doubt, and other times when we must shoulder our boat and concede to the circumstances. This balancing act can be difficult for those wired to achieve at all cost. There's a constant pressure to stack on accomplishments — more rivers, harder sections, cleaner lines, more likes on social media. But it's a yearning that can never be quenched. And this drive for success can compel us to behave recklessly. On the river, it could mean a harmful swim, loss of gear, or drowning. In life, trying to succeed at all costs can lead to broken relationships, financial instability, incarceration, depression, and anxiety. This pressure to succeed can come from different influences. There are times when we feel the need to prove something to ourselves, and other times when we feel peer pressure to fit in with the group.

Whether the source of the stress is internal or external, humility can help keep us from making unnatural and potentially destructive decisions. We need to have confidence in our character and the courage to say "no," even when it is to ourselves.

Ironically, the drive to push beyond our limit can also hold us back. Pressure and stress can cause muscle tightness, inability to focus, and zap precious physical and mental energy. We can counteract this tension by lowering our guard and accepting our limitations. When we open ourselves up to interpreting experiences differently, good things happen. For example, there have been river trips when I would lose touch with the present moment because I was preoccupied with running the bigger nasty stuff downstream. In those moments, my paddling suffered along with my enjoyment of the water because I had put pressure on myself to run everything with no exceptions. As I matured and started to understand my abilities better, I eventually accepted portaging as a tolerable alternative to running every rapid. Acting with humility, I let go of the high expectations I had put on myself. I allowed myself to connect with the present tense and enjoy the river one rapid at a time. This allowed me to tap into the flow much sooner. I was no longer concerned about what rapids roared downstream because I had already allowed myself to consider portaging. By the time I arrived at the rapids in question, I would usually be more relaxed, paddling with more confidence, and I could make a better decision on running it or not. In the recovery community, this is referred to as "One day at a time." It's a reminder to stay present and appreciate where you are in the process. Releasing the pressure we put on ourselves is one aspect that helps us perform at higher levels and moves us toward humility.

The next major step toward humility is accepting that we can't control everything in our lives. A kayaker's independent nature is not unique. The desire to have control and make our own decisions is a universal trait. But this type of behavior can be isolating and a barrier to humility. We have to accept that some things are out of our control. We can't dictate when the snow melts in the spring, and we can't control the actions of others. Humility is about letting go of what we can't control and focusing on what we can — our own thoughts and actions.

Letting go can be very hard for people accustomed to always paddling their own boat and choosing their own lines. There's a certain pride and arrogance that comes with trying to control everything in our lives. Usually, this stems from insecurity. In my case, I desperately needed control of some aspects of my life, because other areas were so chaotic. That chaos made me feel inadequate. To counteract the insecurity, I sought out ways to feel better about myself while ignoring the things I struggled with. The refuge of the river offered me that safe space. And so did drugs and alcohol. As my downward spiral continued, I clung onto the things I could control and neglected the rest. This led to isolation, broken relationships, and depression. Ultimately, I had to admit that I was powerless over many things and that I needed help from others. Drawing on the lessons from kayaking, I needed to figure out how to navigate the rapids and find people to help me.

If we look back at our early days trying to learn a new activity, we see that we were very humble and eager for assistance. We took an inventory of sorts and looked for help from others. We sought out people who were better than us to learn from. When we searched for help, we found it.

When we began kayaking, our newfound paddling buddies guided us down our first rivers, taught us proper techniques, and helped boost our confidence when we were timid. They set up safety for us. They chased down our boats when we swam and helped us drain them on shore. Our mentors on the water were there for us when we needed them. There was no judgment on their side because these acts of kindness were passed down to them as well. Accepting help from others is a rite of passage for all adventurers, and so is giving it. It takes humility to accept and offer help. No one can go through life completely on their own.

We need guides off the river, too. If we can humbly ask for and graciously accept help on the river, what prevents us from transferring humility to the street? For me, it was fear and pride. I was too proud to admit that I was stuck in areas of my life without a clue of how to get unstuck. Fear of being judged kept me from telling people that I was struggling mentally and emotionally. Lucky for me, when I hit rock bottom, I had people there to throw me a rope — just like someone would on a river. I slowly learned that it was OK to ask for help and admit that I didn't know what to do. Just like a novice kayaker would, I sought out people to learn from — mentors, sponsors, teachers, healers. Whatever you want to call them, they now do for me what my paddling buddies have always done: They show me the lines, set safety for me, encourage me when I'm timid, help me drain my boat when I swim, and remind me to keep coming back. Having the humility to ask for help when we need it, and seek out those who can provide it, is essential, whether we need help improving our relationships, controlling our finances, finding sobriety, or transforming any other area of our life. Humility allows us to step outside of ourselves and toward others.

Humility is a foundation we can build on for progression on and off the water. Admit your flaws, work on those areas, and learn from others. If you think

> **Humility allows us to step outside of ourselves and toward others.**

everything is fine, you won't try to develop further. As kayakers, we made the decision to push ourselves and take action. Want to go from learning to paddle in a pool to the river? Learn how to roll and brace. Want to step up from Class III to Class IV? Dial in that boof and eddy hopping. Want to paddle Class V? Center your life around kayaking. As boaters, we understand and accept this fact — that there's so much to learn and that we can't do it all on our own. We come into this sport as humble as can be.

But in the real world, admitting our flaws and asking for help is difficult. Pride and ignorance can be barriers from progressing toward a happier and healthier life. I know so many people, who got stuck in the same thrill-seeking patterns of their 20s. They form an identity based on the labels of the lifestyle they choose — kayaker, ski bum, partyer, dirtbag. Those labels become their identity, and they surround themselves with people and circumstances that support this belief. They never progress in life because they don't realize they can. I know because I was that way.

On many occasions, I disgruntledly told my wife as I walked out the door for yet another long weekend of paddling, "You married a kayaker. This is how it is." What a bunch of dismissive, self-centered bullshit that was. It wasn't until my world fell apart and I was forced to rebuild, that I realized I could create my new life any way I wanted to. I didn't have to identify as a specific label any longer. I wasn't just some kayaker living the dirtbag lifestyle. I could be a great husband. I could be a sharp businessman. I could get sober. And I could still have fun in my boat. Now instead of reinforcing my belief that "I'm a kayaker and this is how it is," I remind myself that "I'm a considerate and loving husband who takes care of his family." That takes humility. It's not just about me anymore.

The realization that I could rebuild my life put me back at the starting point — it was just like arriving at a put-in to run a river for the second time. But I had to swallow my pride and take accountability. I couldn't hide behind my self-indulgent identity any longer. I needed to face the fact that other areas of my life needed my attention more than kayaking did. Instead of fighting the current, I had to work with the flow of everyday responsibilities. As I did when I was a beginner boater, I approached this fresh start with humility. I had to figure out where I wanted to go, who could help me get there, and what new skills I needed to learn. If I could manage to go from paddling in swimming pools to hucking waterfalls, certainly I could apply these lessons in humility to other aspects of my life as well.

CHAPTER 04

RESILIENCE

"Except when you don't.
Because, sometimes, you won't.
I'm sorry to say so
but, sadly, it's true
that Bang-ups
and Hang-ups
can happen to you."
— **Dr. Seuss,** *Oh, the Places You'll Go!*

TRACTOR'S HEAVY GUITAR CHORDS along with our booming voices filled the big Montana night sky. The lyrics were like a battle cry for a group of triumphant warriors who had fought a personal war. A team of survivors who fought cancer at an age when they should have been out running and playing with other kids. Instead, they spent summers in hospital rooms, missed their proms, and had years taken from them and their families.

While each participant had their own unique story of battling cancer and came from different parts of the country, they had all assembled that week in Montana with one common goal — to learn how to whitewater kayak. If they could survive cancer, surely they could handle a week on the river. For them, the week would be a lesson in paddling. For me, the week would be a lesson in what resilience truly means.

—Excerpt from the chapter "Out Living It: Moccasin to West Glacier, Middle Fork of the Flathead" on page 122

The river of life is a never-ending series of calm and rough waters. If you want to live a happy and healthy life, you need to be able to bounce back from disappointments, surprises, and traumas that life is guaranteed to dish out. It's easy to feel confident and happy when the waters are smooth. But when the water gets rough, we can find ourselves in situations that are difficult to recover from. Even when we do our best to navigate challenging rapids, there will be times when we are pulled from our boats and forced to swim for our lives. It's in these moments of crisis when we need to be resilient. Being able to recover

Is there a lesson of resilience that can be learned from those who don't survive?

from the lowest of lows takes a heroic effort, but it can, and must, be done if you want to live a life of contentment.

Sadly, there are also times when success is impossible even with all of the help in the world. Ultimately, we will all be faced with the insurmountable obstacle of death. But it's when death comes too soon that we take pause as a community and reflect. I think of my mom who lost a seven-year battle with Alzheimer's at the young age of 62, soldiers who never returned home from war, and little kids who lost their battles to cancer.

Is there a lesson of resilience that can be learned from those who don't survive? Absolutely.

The lesson is that life is precious and we must make the most of it while we are here; to live a good life and not squander a second chance. Whether it be finding sobriety, being released from prison, or walking away from a near-death experience like drowning, cancer, or war — a second chance is a precious opportunity to change the way you view and live within the world. Not everyone is lucky enough to get a second chance at life. But if you are one of those fortunate few, resilience will be your biggest ally.

When we get knocked down (and everyone does at some point), it's how we get up that determines our future. We can't always control what happens to us, but we can control how we respond. We can also choose to find meaning in the challenges we face. With all of the talk about "getting back up" and "finding meaning," it's easy to fall into the trap of trying to move on too quickly. I'm not suggesting that we push aside any unwanted emotions of sadness or grief when bad things happen. It's important to recognize these feelings and honor them. Holding back any emotion for too long can lead to an unhealthy imbalance, eventually resulting in an explosion or implosion.

> **Like physical therapy can help you overcome a knee injury, cognitive therapy can help you overcome emotional trauma.**

In fact, connecting with our softer side builds self-awareness. We all have a vulnerable inner child who can be scared, timid, sad, or ashamed. Accepting this is an important part of being well-rounded. Even though we've been raised to be tough and not show weakness, sometimes being tough isn't the right thing to do. Sometimes we need to be soft and vulnerable to find the lessons in life. Once we understand this about ourselves, we can be more compassionate and in tune to our own healing process, which is what resilience is all about — healing.

So what does all this inner child mumbo jumbo have to do with resiliency? The lesson is to honor our natural healing process and the associated feelings that come with it. Don't repress or avoid them. Let emotions flow through us like water in a stream. It's by doing so that we allow ourselves to move forward. If we try and repress our feelings, we build an emotional dam that is guaranteed to break one day, flooding us with emotional extremes, then leaving us empty. Last time I checked, kayakers weren't big fans of dams. We prefer free-flowing water. So embrace this small lesson from the river and accept your emotions as they come so that we can live freely.

Just like scar tissue can hinder range of motion after surgery, the psychological scars of our past can prevent us from moving on with our lives. Here's the good news: Both physical and emotional scar tissue can be broken down over time, allowing a person to move through life freely once again. Like physical therapy can help you overcome a knee injury, cognitive therapy can help you overcome emotional trauma. In either case, we can't rush recovery. The body and mind take time to rejuvenate, and it's essential to respect the healing process. It's common practice to walk with crutches and take it easy on a leg after a knee injury. This softer-gentler approach should also be applied when healing from emotional trauma. Just don't get stuck limping along forever. At a certain point, we need to drop the crutches and stand on our own two feet again.

Not taking the proper steps to heal a busted knee

can result in continuous re-injury to the point it becomes incapacitated. This same principle can happen psychologically. A common downward spiral for many people is dwelling on the past and believing that they are a victim of their circumstances, powerless and unaccountable for their future. Like lots of others, I've been trapped in this depressive cycle myself. It usually goes like this: Something traumatic happens, I feel bad about myself, negative self-talk floods my mind, I try to cope in unhealthy ways, which reinforces the negative self-talk, more bad things happen, and so on. This downward spiral is complicated to pull out of, but it can be done.

How does one develop resilience? It starts with mindfulness in action. Here are a few esoteric concepts to develop a resilient mindset: *Our past is over. The future doesn't exist.* The present moment is all we have. It's in the present that we choose how we want our future to be and take action. It's in the present that we can choose to reinterpret our past and find a lesson we can apply. The past does not define our future; our present does. It's not what happens to us that matters; it's how we react. We have to be aware of our mindset, have an intention to move forward, and commit to taking action. With these concepts in mind, you must then ask what you're to do with the present moment — dwell in frustration and sadness of the past, or honor yourself and move forward? Resilient people favor the latter.

Our support community is often an overlooked aspect of resilience. It would be easy to say that with the right attitude, any adversity can be overcome. But that's a lie. Some challenges are too complicated to face on your own.

That's why surrounding yourself with positive people is so important. We need people in our lives who can support us through the difficult times by helping us heal, building our self-esteem, holding us accountable, being honest with us, and pushing us to take the uncomfortable steps associated with rebuilding.

Our support group can be made up of trusted people, including your family, friends, and peer groups. But sometimes we might need people with particular skills. I was physically and emotionally battered after my near fatal swim on Quake Lake. So I sought help from professionals; the ER doctor to stitch up my chin, a dentist to fix my broken teeth, and later a physical therapist to work on my leg and back. There's no way I could have done all that on my own. I needed specialized help so my body would recover. The emotional wounds from that traumatic event were just as painful as my battered body. After I got my face fixed, I needed to get my head right. I could have tried to bury my emotions and ignore the nightmares and anxiety I was experiencing. Instead, I sought out a trauma counselor to help me through the inner turmoil. That experience taught me that being resilient doesn't have to be a lonely battle. Leaning on your community when you need it will help you heal faster than you otherwise would, on your own.

After something horrible happens to us, it's easy to fall into a depressive cycle of wallowing in self-defeat. Resilience isn't just about sucking it up and bouncing back from these hard times. To live a happy and healthy life, we need to take action in order to heal from past wounds. Life's too short and precious to take second chances for granted. Patience and compassion toward ourselves can help with recovery, but we can't get stuck in a rut. At a certain point, we must take action to move on with life. If you can't do it on your own, seek out a support community for help. Resilience teaches us that we can't change the past, but we can find meaning in the lessons, choose how we want our future to be, and take action toward a better life.

CHAPTER 05

FLOW

"Flow follows focus."

— **Steven Kotler**

Joe Booth in Fine Line by Bob Booth

THE SUN SHONE directly overhead as we got in our kayaks below the portage. I felt its heat through my helmet. The river was calm and teeming with life. A recent hatch of hundreds of lacewing swarmed just inches above the surface. Trout jumped, eager for the flying snacks. A bald eagle, alarmed by our colorful boats, leapt from a pine tree and soared over our heads and downstream.

It's in these moments that the magic of the river is felt, not just seen. Unlike hikers along the bank, admiring the scenery from afar, we were within the scenery, part of the river. I felt the water roll down my paddle blade and onto my hands. I watched it soak into my skin. I was part of the river.

This connection to the river stayed with me the entire day. Every ferry, boof, eddy turn, surf, brace, and stroke felt effortless and in tune with the water. I have never paddle so well in my life, and I hope one day I'm able to paddle like that again. I was fully immersed in the flow, present with each ripple of water.

—*Excerpt from the chapter "Keep Coming Back: Hells Canyon, Boulder River, Montana" on page 148*

The sight of a river is never the same for the fortunate boaters who have experienced the mind-bending phenomenon called "flow" while on the water. Once you've experienced this ecstasy, you'll always look at the river differently; searching for lines down the rapids, playing in holes along the way, or admiring the complexity of whitewater. Although it's fleeting, flow feels like an alternate reality where time slows down, and you become a part of the river, balanced delicately within the misty line where the water meets the wind. You're exactly where you're supposed to be, at the perfect moment, sharing space and time with water, rock, and air.

In those moments of flow, your concentration is so deep that you can't tell if the water dripping from your hands is coming from the river or from within you. The answer is both. The water flowing in the river bed also flows through you. You are not just on the river; you have become the river. You haven't tapped into the flow, you have become the flow. You are both current and eddy. You are water and air, rock and tree. You are birds and bugs, sun and sky. You are not in the river; you are the river.

What, exactly, is flow? Let me preface this by stating that flow is something that needs to be experienced to be fully understood. It's an abstract experience; trying to capture it in words can't do it justice. It's like trying to describe what a plum tastes like when it's picked from the tree and eaten at the peak of ripeness. If you've only purchased plums from the store, you'll never know how sweet and delicious they can be. Having had a plum tree in my backyard growing up, I can tell you that there is no comparison. It's the same with flow; difficult to describe, but divine when experienced. Near the end of this chapter,

I offer techniques that can assist with getting into the flow. Perhaps once you have experienced the sensation, you can send me your definition and capture it better than I can (as well as provide your opinion on the sweetness of store-bought plums).

Flow is defined as "an optimal state of consciousness where we feel and perform our best." It can be described as a state of immersion so intense that awareness is heightened to the point of connection or "oneness" with your surroundings. It's blended relaxation and alertness. When you are in the zone, you're pushed to your limits, but able to perform masterfully. You can focus intensely on the critical task, blocking out all distractions, feeling confident, and moving smoothly through space and time.

Also known as "being in the zone," flow is one of the most sought-after experiences a human can obtain. This heightened experience isn't just for action sports enthusiasts. We see many different examples of flow in our daily lives. For instance, an artist who is absorbed into the canvas they paint, a basketball player who scores a 50-point game, a gardener who spends all day working in their garden not realizing they haven't stopped for hours, or an office worker sucked into their computer screen intensely focused on their project. We lose track of time, block out all distractions, and concentrate deeply but effortlessly. When we're in the flow, we're working hard and in an almost euphoric state.

So what's going on here? What causes us to feel like we are becoming one with the infinite universe? Time for another quick lesson in kayaker neuroscience.

In the flow state, the brain goes through a series of complex physiological changes. The trance-like experience is partially due to brainwaves slowing down along with some other trippy brain activity. Usually, when we are awake, our brain is surfing fast-charging beta waves that keep us alert. In flow, however, we slow to the day-dreaming waves of alpha and the REM sleep waves of theta, allowing us to glide smoothly between thoughts. The colossal rush associated with being in the zone is caused by large quantities of norepinephrine, dopamine, endorphins, anandamide, and serotonin simultaneously pumping through our blood. The flow state is one of the only times our bodies experience such a euphoric concoction of pleasure hormones. Lastly, the brain goes through "transient hypofrontality." This fancy term is the temporary slowing down of your brain's frontal lobe, the part of the brain primarily in charge of problem-solving, judgment, perception of time, and perception of self. So think about all of this happening at the same time: Our brainwaves slow down, pleasure hormones spike, and we lose our capacity to interpret time and self. These interwoven processes allow us to concentrate, lose ourselves in the moment, remove judgment, and absorb information as it comes.

Because flow has such a euphoric effect but is elusive and fleeting nature, those who have experienced it often spend much of their time and effort trying to replicate it. Many people I know — myself included — have exhibited the addictive chase of the next perfect line or wave, dedicating entire chunks of our lives toward the pursuit. The feeling is so satisfying and addicting that it's no wonder people try to replicate it with mind-altering substances like drugs and alcohol. While this can be a problem for junkies who get addicted to the rush, it can also be a good thing for those who understand that being in the zone isn't just for thrillseekers trying to escape reality. When the same principles are applied to our day-to-day lives, flow offers many advantages: Our concentration improves, our ability to connect with others increases, we're more likely to complete tasks, and we feel better about ourselves. Overall, flow contributes to a life worth living.

So how do we get in the zone and achieve peak performance? As the action sports journalist turned flow researcher Steven Kotler puts it, "Flow follows focus." Where we place our attention will determine where our energy will go.

As we all know, it's much easier to focus on a task when we enjoy the activity. Doing something you enjoy has many therapeutic effects and routinely immersing yourself in recreation can help you be a happier person. Whether you're gardening, kayaking, painting, meditating, jogging, or writing, it's possible to reach a flow state. The key is to find an activity that can hold your deep concentration with the right combination of enjoyment and challenge. This balancing point between arousal and relaxation is where "the zone" exists. Consistently putting yourself in the zone will help you reach higher levels of performance and confidence. When you're in flow, you're challenged to the peak of your ability level, but able to maintain control and fluidity. Eventually, your comfort zone will expand because your skills have improved, and by default, your ability to take on more significant challenges.

So why do so many people get hooked on adrenaline sports like kayaking? Research indicates that getting in the zone can be triggered more rapidly with activities that quickly demand your full attention and mimic a fight or flight response. This is why action sports are most often associated with flow. As risk increases, so does our focus and attention. It turns out that our brain's natural Fight, Flight or Freeze response is a precursor to the flow state.

Flow might be an evolutionary byproduct of the survival situations our ancestors faced. Millions of years ago, making it from one day to the next was all that mattered. To survive, we had to hunt and scavenge for our food while simultaneously trying not to be food for something hunting us. There was no time for checking Facebook and posting selfies on Instagram. We had to maintain an intense focus that would allow us another day on Earth.

This extremely stressful lifestyle of flight or fight did have some perks. For example, outrunning a saber-toothed tiger or killing a woolly mammoth would have lead to one of the most epic adrenaline rushes ever — an X-Games gold-medal status adrenaline rush. But unlike modern thrillseekers who live for the next big rush, our ancestors who survived passed down their genes because of the rush. If those early extreme athletes didn't have the focus and skills required to survive in their dangerous world, none of us would be here today. That ability to focus and achieve a monumental task, like taking down a wooly mammoth, is precisely the type of thing we experience in the flow state.

Lucky for us, we don't have to outrun a prehistoric beast to experience flow. We don't even need to put ourselves in a risky fight or flight scenario like kayaking. We can direct our focus to any goal-oriented activity that's both challenging and pleasurable. In those situations, it is crucial that we can concentrate. And the best way to focus is by eliminating distractions.

One of the problems of distractions is that they take up precious mental bandwidth. Scientists estimate that the human brain is only able to process about 120 bits of information per second. Once you hit that 120-bit threshold, the ability to absorb and understand information begins to break down. To put that in context, holding a conversation with one person requires around 60 bits per second — well under the 120-bit limit. But the bandwidth gets used up quickly once you throw in distractions. For example, trying to understand two people talking to you at the same time is extremely difficult, and trying to hold three conversations simultaneously is impossible. As more distractions enter the equations, our ability to concentrate becomes more difficult.

Think of this bandwidth issue like a log-jammed river. Without obstruction, the water in the stream moves freely

We have to get rid of the trapped wood in our minds and our surroundings.

downstream. But when a big log gets snagged on a rock, the water has to redirect around and through the trunk and branches. As the log sits in the river, it traps more sticks, branches, and other logs floating in the stream. Eventually, the log and all of its collected driftwood create a log jam. The water no longer flows freely downstream. Instead, it builds up behind the log jam, flushing through any small opening it can find. What was once a free-flowing body of water is now a damn.

In this metaphor, the free-flowing water is our ability to concentrate, and the log jam is all of the distractions in our lives. We can't just add more water and expect our same level of performance. We need to eliminate distractions. We have to get rid of the trapped wood in our minds and our surroundings.

Eliminating distractions would be impossible if the brain didn't have a filtration system known as the Reticular Activating System (RAS). We can't handle the millions of bits of information our senses take in per second. So our RAS acts like a bouncer at a nightclub, standing guard to decide which 120 bits get access to our consciousness. By analyzing the context of everything we experience in every living moment, this complex neurological system makes split-second decisions on what is relevant and what can be blocked out. By doing so, the RAS plays a significant role in how we see ourselves and experience the world around us. If we train our brains to think constant distractions are a good thing, then the RAS will welcome them in. However, if we practice focusing our attention on specific goals, then the RAS will block out the things that don't support the new directive. For example, when you scout a rapid, you're able to filter the complexity of the environment to a series of patterns that show you a safe line. In this scenario, you wouldn't be distracted by the leaves on the trees, sand along the bank, or wet booties on your feet. All of these things are within your sensory perception, but you only focus on what matters at the moment — the line down the rapid. That's your RAS doing its job.

In our modern world, we are bombarded with distractions — partying with friends, trips and adventures, TV, YouTube, social media, notifications, texts, work demands, relationships, swiping left, swiping right. We become accustomed to this type of busy lifestyle filled with distractions, and then we wonder why there aren't enough hours in the day to get anything meaningful done. Living everyday like this trains our brain to jump from one shiny object to the next. As discussed in the chapter on Commitment, the brain wants to follow the path of least resistance. Whatever you establish as your default operating mode is what your mind will crave. So if you continuously allow yourself to be overtaken by distractions, then you'll crave stimulus even when none are present. One of the harmful impacts of this neural overload is that we slowly lose the ability to focus. When we need to sit quietly and concentrate, our brain will resist the silence in search of stimulation, making it difficult to focus and nearly impossible to get into the flow when we need to.

It turns out, that's precisely what the brain does when we are in the flow — it eliminates distractions. By removing the log jam in our minds, we can reach a state of concentration that leads to peak performance. Our brains do this through a series of complex processes that allow us to tap into a primitive yet sophisticated mindset which rewards us with the feeling of euphoria. An advantage of flow-inducing activities like kayaking is, they demand immediate attention. The downside is, there's potential for injury or death. If you want to get into the flow, but you're not willing to take that risk or aren't in a position to grab your boat and huck a waterfall, an alternative is to eliminate distractions and do something you enjoy that also stretches out of your comfort zone.

By participating in activities that both challenge and satisfy us, we can reach higher levels of personal performance and accomplish our goals. Apply this practice of flow to your everyday routines. Don't shy away from challenges just because you don't enjoy them. Shift your mindset and view challenges as opportunities to sharpen your concentration and your ability to follow through. Every day, life provides us with opportunities to practice flow, view obstacles as opportunities, and connect deeply with the world around us. With this understanding, we realize that we aren't just living in the world, we are a part of it.

FROM
THE
RIVER

CHAPTER 06

A CALLING:

Tunnel Chute, Middle Fork American River

"The mountains are calling and I must go."
— John Muir

A CALLING. That's what I felt when I was a little boy flipping through my dad's copy of *California Whitewater*, the classic guidebook by Jim Cassady and Fryar Calhoun. The cover shot of the book is a group of early 1980s-era rafters dropping into the bottom hole of Tunnel Chute rapid on the Middle Fork of the American River. Tunnel Chute ends with this pounding drop into a steep, boat-eating hole. As a boy, the image both terrified and inspired me.

The cover photo of *California Whitewater* captures the moment of truth frequently lost in the modern culture of GoPro POV on YouTube and Instagram. Frozen in time, the group of brave paddlers sits poised on the precipice, fully committed, digging in deep with their paddles, staring forever into the gut of one of nature's most powerful and violent gifts: whitewater. It's the moment in time which every serious paddler lives for — that moment of truth when your line, your attitude, your preparation, and the nature of the river all culminate in an instant that can't be taken back. You are entirely committed and fully present.

The river called to me through the lens that captured this photo, this was my moment of truth. And by doing so, the river redirected the course of my life like a boulder in the middle of a stream redirects the current.

The first time I saw that picture, I remember lying awake that night thinking Tunnel Chute was waiting for me, calling for me. I could hear it thunder and crash. And I knew someday, I would have to run that drop. I knew I would be in the very same spot as those rafters staring into the maw of the river. What I didn't know at the time was, the life lessons I would learn from the sport would prepare me for some of the biggest challenges I would face later in my life.

FROM THE RIVER

Nearly two decades after seeing Tunnel Chute on the cover of *California Whitewater*, I would put in on the Middle Fork of the American River and find myself sitting in an eddy above the rapid that had been calling me. I had committed to run the rapid as a boy, and here I stood as a young man. Because it was so deeply imprinted on me as a kid, I quickly recalled the image of the rafters on the lower drop. But studying the entire rapid in person was quite a different experience. This was before the days of YouTube scouting (Yes, I'm that old), so it was the first time I had seen any more of the rapid than just the bottom hole in the photo. I remember feeling overwhelmed. I expected to see water rushing down a stream culminating in a big hole at the bottom. Instead, the rapid was a weird blend of a man-made spillway and natural erosion channels cascading onto one another, causing a cacophony of lateral waves and manky holes. It wasn't like any other rapid I had ever seen or run before.

After the scout, I walked up to my boat to fulfill the destiny of my younger self — that little boy who was lured into kayaking by an amazing photo. There was no time to feel sentimental or contemplate the mysteries of the universe that led me to this point. My adrenaline was pumping, and I was focused on staying upright through the ugly rapid.

Shortly after I tucked myself into my kayak and pulled out of the eddy, I had run the drop and answered the call of the river. The moments in between were fast-paced, turbulent, and ended with a quick roll while I flushed out of the bottom hole of Tunnel Chute.

Two decades of anticipation led me to this point. And it was all over in less than 30 seconds. The river beckoned me as a child, and I had finally satisfied my yearning to put myself on the very precipice that the rafters on the book's cover had been sitting on since I was a kid.

As I floated into the dark tunnel cut into the bedrock below Tunnel Chute, heart still pounding with adrenaline, I looked back up at the drop with a strong sense of pride. I pictured that group of rafters hanging over the ledge as if they were permanent fixtures on the river. I identified with them more now. I felt like I had finally joined their tribe. The shadow cast by the tunnel seemed to act like a "fade to black" at a movie's end. Within moments I could no longer see Tunnel Chute and the current redirected my attention to the next horizon line. This is how it goes on the river and in life.

Follow your calling. You will know when your calling is real because it will speak to a part of you that you didn't even realize exists.

RIVER GUIDE

"THERE'S GOLD IN THEM THAR HILLS!" In 1848 gold was discovered on the South Fork American River, triggering a surge of 300,000 people making their way into California looking to stake their claim and strike it rich. Many of the rivers and streams in the area were permanently scarred by the impact of the Gold Rush — including the Middle Fork of the American, which felt the effects of blasting, mining, and dredging that would forever change the river's banks.

Legend has it that one playful and clever gold panner, Zeek Gentile, talked his buddies into redirecting the river by blasting a giant tunnel through a hill. With his infectious laugh and knack for talking people into his schemes, Zeek convinced his mining crew that blasting would give them easier access to gold on the riverbed and the ore locked within the ridge. So blast they did.

It's said that the moment water started flowing through the tunnel, Zeek was hypnotized by the river and couldn't resist the temptation to get the first descent on Tunnel Chute. He turned to his mining buddies, let out a high-pitched snicker and spoke his iconic last words, "Hold my pan and watch this!" Zeek jumped on top of his rinky-dink wooden raft and styled the rapid cleaner than a polished nugget of 24 karat gold, laughing hysterically the entire time.

Mysteriously, Zeek never came out the other side of the tunnel after making it through the rapid unscathed. His gold mining buddies believed that his soul became trapped in the tunnel as punishment for blasting through the ridge. To this day, if you call his name while floating through the dark void you can still hear echoes of his laughter.

As the result of Zeek's fateful water diversion project during the Gold Rush, Tunnel Chute is a man-made channel about 15 feet wide and 200 feet long. The blast formed a deep, long, and narrow slot that redirects the river literally into a tunnel through the bedrock of the mountain. The variable rock angle caused by the blasting result in powerful lateral waves that want to push your nose into the wall as you make your way toward the thunderous compression hole at the bottom.

Only a mile and a half into the run, Tunnel Chute demands immediate respect and attention. Scout on the right when you come to the massive horizon line that disappears into a hill. From the put-in below the dam, a few pool-drop rapids give you a chance to physically and mentally prepare yourself for a wild ride.

There are about four or five Class III-IV rapids after Tunnel Chute, and then the action slows down for about nine miles of scenic flatwater and Class II. The beautiful wilderness canyon offers several camping sites available for those with a camping permit.

A wide horizon line marks the beginning of the next whitewater section beginning with the Class IV drop, Chunder. Take out river-right immediately at the next horizon line. This is the Class V+, Ruck-a-Chucky Falls — a giant boulder pile at most flows that provides a slim line for rafters to send their boats down. There's certainly potential to kayak this drop, but safety would be difficult, and the flows would need to be ideal to avoid getting sucked under the rocks and into an underwater sieve. A well-established portage on river right makes the decision easy for most paddlers.

After Ruck-a-Chucky, the rapids continue for another few miles to the take-out.

State: **California**
River: **Middle Fork of the American**
Section: **Tunnel Chute**
Difficulty: **III-IV+ (V+)**
Flow: **500-3,000 cfs**
Distance: **16.5 miles**
Gradient: **25 fpm**

Take-Out: Ruck-a-Chucky Campsite is located about 10 miles northeast of Auburn, California. Head east on Foresthill Road for about 8 miles then turn right on Drivers Flat Road. A little less than half a mile down Drivers Flat, veer left at the fork in the dirt road. This becomes Old Greenwood Bridge Road and your take-out will be down about two miles. *38.962585, -120.932194*

Put-In: About an hour from the take-out, Indian Bar River Access is directly below the Oxbow Reservoir. From Ruck-a-Chucky Campsite, head back up to Foresthill Road and go right. On Foresthill Road, go east for 9 miles to the town of Foresthill.

Turn right on Mosquito Ridge Road and follow it for 11 miles to T in the road. Go right at the T onto FR 23. About a mile down, hang a right at the next T onto Rubicon Road. Indian Bar will be about .7 miles down the hill. *39.005970, -120.747413*

CHAPTER 07

WE ARE ALL BETWEEN SWIMS:

Tobin, North Fork Feather River

"Everyone has a plan until they get punched in the face."
— **Mike Tyson**

Kevin's Gate by Dave Steindorf

SITTING IN a calm eddy above a difficult rapid can be a lonely place of contemplation. It's in the safety of this pool that the decision must be made to paddle or portage. You're the only one who can determine whether or not you successfully navigate the water. Even if you've scouted the rapid with the help of your fellow boaters, watched as other kayakers made it down with style, and you have friends in safety positions along the river's banks — for a moment it's just you and the river. The result depends on your willingness to put in the effort necessary to succeed. Even with all of the preparation and excitement of running the rapid, you're not fully committed until you've crossed the boiling eddy-line separating the calm pool from the swift and powerful current. The eddy-line represents the barrier which divides those who are willing to follow through with their plans and the others who sit and dream about goals they aren't willing to work for. There's no turning back once you cross that line, you either navigate the challenging water or suffer the consequences of failure.

Whitewater kayaking is an emotionally and physically demanding activity. For every paddler there comes a time when he or she is faced with the ultimate question: "Do I get back in my boat or not?" This seems like a simple question. Kayaking is fun, so why wouldn't they want to get back in their boat? This dilemma of whether to continue is usually asked after the river hands you a beatdown. You've crawled out of the cold water, you're soaking wet, exhausted from the swim, knees and shins bleeding, shaken physically and emotionally, and...there are more rapids downstream waiting to pull you back in. Fear and doubt creep into your head.

Before you decide to get back in your boat or not, you run through a series of questions: How many more rapids do we have until the take-out? Am I good enough to finish the run or am I going to die? Is this even fun anymore? What will my friends think if I don't get back in my boat? How far is the hike to the cars? Do I even want to be a kayaker anymore? How come everyone is better than me? Are they really going to make me drink beer out of my bootie because I swam? These are the doubts and questions that run through your head while you sit soaking wet on the river bank.

Or maybe you contemplate these thoughts from bed at night. You are exhausted from the day, road-weary from the long shuttle, strung out on the stress hormone cortisol, embarrassed that you were the only one in your crew who swam, sore from the long day of paddling, legs bruised from swimming over rocks, stomach still sour from the bootie beers. Wondering why you put yourself through these types of things you ask yourself, is kayaking still worth it?

It's in these moments of fear and doubt that the kayaker's destiny takes shape.

Many paddlers decide to walk away from the sport after their first significant swim. They determine the risk is not worth the reward. There's no shame in walking away from kayaking forever and selling your boat on Craigslist. Many people do. That's why you see so many paddlers drop-out when they progress into Class III and feel what it's like to get beat down by the river. Sure, a quick Class II swim to shore is scary and exhausting, but a swim down a long Class III rapid is enough to make a lot of people run for the couch.

But for others, swimming is part of the experience. Getting trashed by the river is an accepted risk worth the reward of going places only kayakers can go. Learning how to battle in a rapid while remaining calm takes time. To these paddlers, a swim is viewed as a lesson in humility which results in the practice of resilience. For those who develop and maintain the necessary physical

A swim is viewed as a lesson in humility which results in the practice of resilience.

and psychological fitness to continue paddling, the river opens up and reveals more and more about itself. You will see and experience wonders only bestowed to kayakers. Equally important, the river teaches you more and more about yourself — lessons that will positively impact other areas of your life. As always, the river is the ultimate teacher, reminding us to remain humble yet confident, and that, as in life, we are all between swims.

FROM THE RIVER

I was exhausted and defeated, but I could see the bridge. One more rapid to go, swim or not, and I'd finally be able to get off the water and be done with my first Class V run, Tobin on the North Fork of California's Feather River.

To say my day hadn't gone as planned would be an understatement. I intended to achieve ultimate glory and finally claim the label of "Class V kayaker." What happened that afternoon was the exact opposite. The river kicked my ass every chance it had and gave me a swim lesson no lifeguard would ever sanction.

As the run began, a simple conversation with a random kayaker foreshadowed my first Class V experience. As we approached the horizon line, he looked at me with a big smile and exclaimed, "Boof it!" To which I replied, "What's a boof?" Moments later I would be swimming. By the end of the day, I swam three times.

I'd never paddled water like Tobin before: a boulder-choked run with ledge after ledge and a continuous current between each drop. I was confident in my Class IV skills, having made easy work of a Class IV run just the day before. But Tobin, a Class V-, was a big step up and demanded a skillset I hadn't developed yet.

So there I was, one rapid into the run and already with a swim. Embarrassed and slightly concerned, I paddled on. On the next rapid I made it a point to get out of my boat and scout. It looked simple enough from the bank; a zig-zag pool-drop rapid that flushed into a generous moving eddy. I knew it had the potential to flip me, but the size of the eddy gave me confidence. Flip me it did. I attempted my roll multiple times, but for some reason, I wasn't able to get up. So there I was swimming again. Frustrated, I self-rescued. When I went to empty my boat, I realized that my drain plug was missing. This had caused my boat to fill with water, which probably affected my ability to roll. Rookie move.

Regardless of the reason, now I was two swims in with a lot of river to go. I had no drain plug, and was pissed off, embarrassed and angry with myself, and worried that my crew was going to leave me to hitchhike to the take-out. I had to get this situation under control.

A little duct tape fixed my drain plug problem, and an auto-boof on the next rapid helped my confidence. "So that's what a boof feels like!" I thought to myself. The light bulbs turned on, and I was able to navigate the middle portion of the run with modest success, battling the rapids and hitting multiple combat rolls. My confidence was booming, but I was exhausted.

At the next significant rapid a few people from my crew hopped out to take a quick look. I should have done so, too. But I was exhausted, and the thought of climbing out of and back into my boat was daunting. Moments later I was swimming for the third time that day. This one was nasty — a long flush over rocks and through multiple holes. Luckily, someone was able to get a rope to me before I swept into the next set of rapids.

I was defeated, freezing cold, energy zapped, confidence stripped, shins bleeding.

The walk down the bank to my boat was one of shame. Negative self-talk flooded my head — "Loser," "Weak,"

"Less than," "Disappointment," "Liability." By the time I got to my boat, I had convinced myself that I was a worthless piece of shit and that no one wanted me on the river.

But then something happened. The resilience and determination I had developed over the years of kayaking started to surface. Hiding the tears in my eyes, I got back into my boat. I peeled across the eddy line and back into the current. There was no pep talk. No motivational music. Just me and the river. I had made it this far and knew I could make it to the end if I just got back in my boat and kept paddling. It was no one's choice but my own. And I had made my decision to stay on the water.

The sun was low in the sky as we came up to the last rapid. I could see the green bridge in the distance, appearing black against the orange sky. I decided that I wasn't going to get out of my boat to scout the last drop. I no longer feared swimming nor embarrassment. All I cared about was finishing the run. I vaguely remember listening to the directions from the people who scouted the line. "Right, left, right, blah, blah, blah." I went numb as I peeled out of the eddy above the final drop. The rapid itself was like a bar fight. The river threw a flurry of punches from every direction and flipped me. But I rolled back up. And as quickly as it began, it ended.

As I floated under the bridge marking the completion of the section, I felt a sense of pride and humility. I had finished the run. The type of paddler that made me was irrelevant. What mattered was that after repeated swims I had gotten back into my boat. I didn't let fear or self-doubt hold me back from accomplishing my goal.

Fourteen years later I returned to Tobin a different

man. I had many Class V sections under my belt, more swims than I'd like to admit, and a completely new perspective on life and kayaking. Between the years on Tobin, I had matured both as a paddler and as a person. Along with a solid boof, I had also developed a new appreciation for second chances. I'd use that boof to paddle a clean run down Tobin, gaining redemption for the humiliation I experienced nearly a decade and a half earlier. Redemption runs like that feel great. As I floated under the bridge at the take-out, the feeling of humility I experienced my first time down was still there. But it was accompanied by a newfound sense of pride for getting back in my boat way back when I was scared and had every reason to give up on the river and myself.

LIFE LESSON

Humility and confidence are often found in unexpected places. Sometimes the outcome we're dealt offers more value than the one we were hoping would transpire.

RIVER GUIDE

Kenya Otto in Tobin

THE NORTH FORK OF THE FEATHER is a wonderful
example of what can happen when private citizens and
corporate interests work together. What was once a
suffering river bed, stripped of its water to power hydro-
projects in the 1950s and 1960s, is now a thriving river
community of anglers and paddlers. This transformation
wouldn't have been possible without local paddlers and
the non-profit American Whitewater teaming up with
utility conglomerate Pacific Gas and Electric. Although it
took more than 15 years of negotiations, the North Fork of
the Feather now offers consistent flows and excellent river
access. Scheduled releases from Rock Creek Dam between
June and October provide some of the most convenient

summertime Class III-V kayaking in California.

With multiple stretches of quality whitewater, Tobin sits in the middle of it all. Upstream is Roger's Flat (III), and downstream is Lobin (IV). Tobin is a boulder-choked run that feels like you are kayaking through a maze. Huge granite rocks create continuous powerful ledge drops, twisting rapids, and sieves. Because of its boulder garden nature, many of Tobin's features are hidden behind rocks and horizon lines. This can make boat scouting difficult for paddlers unfamiliar with the run. But there are plenty of scouting options along the rocky banks and convenient road scouting while you run shuttle.

Although Tobin is only about a mile long, it contains about 10 notable rapids ranging from III+ to V-. The section between the put-in and the double bridge crossing is mainly pool drop, which allows for a good set of warm-up rapids before the action starts. Once you float beneath the double bridges, the gradient increases quickly with "Kevin's Gate." This rapid was named after Kevin Lewis, an American Whitewater paddling ambassador whose commitment to getting flows on the North Fork Feather River was instrumental. Once you pass through Kevin's Gate, Tobin becomes a boulder-choked maze and the rapids stack on top of each other in quick succession until you reach the take-out at the Rock Crest Bridge. You can take out here or continue downstream to the Class IV Lobin run.

State: California
River: North Fork Feather
Section: Tobin
Difficulty: V-
Flow: 300-2,000 cfs
Gauge: AW NF FEATHER R BL ROCK CREEK DIV DAM
Distance: 1.25 miles
Gradient: 150 ft/mi

Take-Out: The turnout for parking is at the greenish Rock Crest Bridge about 40 miles northeast of Oroville, California, on the Feather River Highway (Hwy 70). *39.925799, -121.315420*

Put-In: About 1.3 miles upstream from the take-out, look for a large parking area nestled in the trees between river-right and the highway. *39.939619, -121.309072*

CHAPTER 08

WISE OLD RIVER SHARK

Burnt Ranch Gorge, Trinity River

"Do not go gentle into that good night,
Old age should burn and rave at close of day;
Rage, rage against the dying of the light."
— Dylan Thomas

DRIFT BOATS, campsites, and RVs. These are suitable places for old men with stiff necks and aching backs, on the verge of their golden years. Violent torrents of Class V whitewater are no place for such men. Or are they? In my 30-plus years on the water, I've seen a handful of our wrinkled elders gracefully slide off the rocky banks and into the current. These old paddlers are known as the River Sharks. They usually sport faded vertical-slat life jackets that wouldn't float a watermelon, dry tops in faded purple or blue with traces of glue on the gaskets from years of repairs, and cracking rubber-soled neoprene booties with the side zip and velcro straps. The lines on their faces, leather skin and sun-bleached knuckles are as weathered as the river banks they stand on. The River Sharks pioneered our sport, claimed first descents,

Bob Booth on Rainbow Falls circa 1980

87

named our rapids, and wrote our guide books. There was no checking flows online, no YouTube scouting an entire run in five minutes, no on-demand GoPro footage, and no Instagram or facebook fame from your non-paddling friends/followers. Their knowledge and pioneering spirit have been passed down to us, one paddle stroke at a time through black and white photos and VHS tapes. Much respect should be offered to the River Sharks, and much can be learned from them.

A River Shark raised me. And unless you're pro-kayaker Dane Jackson, showing up at the put-in for a Class V run with your grey-haired dad will get you some concerning looks. Unlike Dane, my dad isn't a world-famous kayaker. He's just a retired weekend warrior who loved to paddle and passed that love down to me. Most guys would be embarrassed by having an old dude following them down the river all the time. Honestly, I was embarrassed too. I wanted to fit in with the cool guys my own age, but the River Shark circling my boat made me stand out. I wanted to be part of the crew, instead of the guy with the goofy dad. But my embarrassment would turn into pride the moment we would get in the water, and my dad would be the first person spinning 360s in holes, catching eddy after eddy, and lacing rapids. He can read water like nobody I've ever met, which allows him to scout rapids in half the time as other guys and find seams in the current that most people couldn't recognize. While he may have been the "old guy" at the put-in, he quickly turned into an elder on the river who made people feel confident.

Lesson learned: Don't judge an old book by its worn-out cover. The content within is what matters.

River Sharks like my dad, or "Bob" as my brother and

I call him, were more keenly connected to the river than paddlers these days. This ability was partially due to the era of equipment they learned with. Another elder of our sport, Mike Garcia, owner of the local river store Northern Lights Trading Co. in Bozeman, Montana, once explained it to me this way: "Boats back then forced the paddler to 'slice and dice' their way down rapids. Kayaks weren't built like they are today — to 'tank' their way down the river, staying upright through anything." This was indeed the case for Bob's 1982 Perception Dancer, which wasn't designed to send boofs, splat rocks, and resurface like modern creek boats. Paddlers from the River Sharks' era had to choose their lines carefully and paddle them flawlessly. There was less room for error, which meant these kayakers needed to see and feel the water at a much more sensitive level.

Lesson learned: Don't rely on equipment, feel the river around you.

Another reason Bob was able to excel at the art of whitewater kayaking was that he was a dedicated student. I didn't realize this aspect of Bob's paddling practice until I asked to borrow his copy of William Nealy's iconic book *Kayak: The Animated Manual of Intermediate and Advanced Whitewater Technique.* Bob led me to a crowded shelf holding over a dozen worn-out volumes of kayaking instruction manuals, swiftwater rescue books, and river guides dating back to the '70s. All of them with dog-eared pages scribbled handwritten notes and highlighted text. That peek into my dad's library made me realize that he had probably read more about kayaking than anyone I knew, certainly more than I had. This explained his uncanny ability to decipher complicated rapids and his plethora of unconventional, but effective, paddle strokes. He had a very balanced theoretical understanding and practical application of paddling. In other words, Bob's kayaking IQ was off the charts.

Lesson learned: Take the time to study the subject you want to master.

FROM THE RIVER

Burnt Ranch Gorge. It was legendary around our kitchen table growing up as a kid. Bone-chilling stories of river glory in this deep rock canyon made for hold-your-fork dinner theater at my house. My brother and I couldn't get enough. Bob basked in the triumph. My mom rolled her eyes.

Fifteen years after first hearing about Burnt Ranch, I'd find myself second in line of a two-pickup caravan heading northbound on I-5. I was listening to a tape of Willie Nelson's greatest hits. Our convoy consisted of my dad and me, kayaks strapped proudly on top of our camper shells. Just as he passed down his love of kayaking, he also passed down his appreciation of pickup trucks with a matching camper shell and do-it-yourself roof rack. We were heading to the place of legend, Burnt Ranch Gorge.

The lyrics of Willie's "Blue Eyes Crying in the Rain" gave me pause. Would I be crying on this run like I had spilled tears of frustration and disappointment earlier on Tobin? Was Willie Nelson somehow foreshadowing my demise with his lyrics "When we kissed goodbye and parted, I knew we'd never meet again"?

The water sloshing around in my right ear brought my mind and eyes back to my speeding pickup on I-5. The water trapped in my head and butterflies in my stomach were an annoying reminder of the Tobin swim fest two hours earlier. Bob witnessed my beating that day on the North Fork Feather. Unlike me, he managed to stay in his boat the entire run, except when quickly jumping out to billy-goat along the bank and scout the lines for his son. I was sure that his encouragement to paddle Burnt Ranch Gorge was either punishment or a death sentence for the embarrassment I had caused him that day. But he assured me I'd be fine. He said he knew every line and I could portage anything I wanted. I figured I'd portage the entire thing. No way was I going to end up dead like Willie Nelson's lyrics were suggesting.

The next day, we were the only ones at the put-in, which was a stark contrast from the crowd of boaters that showed up on the North Fork Feather for the scheduled release the day before. Being alone at the put-in made me nervous. Not that crowds of people somehow make Class V any easier to paddle, but it's comforting seeing other people doing crazy shit, too. My nerves calmed as I got into the flow on the first mile and a half leading up to the gorge. Bob made me practice my roll a bunch. Given my performance on Tobin the day before, I couldn't blame him for encouraging me to get back to the fundamentals. It worked. I was confident, stoked, and running everything clean. Hitting rolls when I needed them and powering through everything we came upon. My confidence was booming. I thought, "Fuck you, Willie Nelson. My blue eyes aren't crying today."

We paddled the majority of the run by ourselves until we happened upon two kayaks stowed on the left bank above a major horizon. Then we noticed two kayakers in their twenties staring into the river as if they were trying to solve calculus problems in their heads. They were pointing at features, looking at each other with concern, and scratching their heads. The rapid they were scouting was Middle Burnt Ranch Falls. Deep into the run, it's a stout Class V requiring multiple moves around boulders, holes, and slides.

As we got out of our boats to scout, they watched us approach. Sizing up my grey-haired dad with skepticism, they asked us how our day was going. Bob read these two bros like an old pro. Without even looking at the river he spoke softly with confidence, "I'll run it on the right if you guys want to follow me down." Their eyes got as wide as saucers, and their faces revealed what they were obviously thinking — "Who is this old dude that thinks he can solve our calculus equation without even looking at the paper?" Keep in mind that Bob's usually the oldest thing on the river except the rocks and trees hugging the bank. You can't blame these young guns for being skeptical of a River Shark.

Bob looked at me and said the words I'd heard a hundred times before. "Joseph, watch me run it and then decide if you want to." Like an old scruffy college professor in front of a class of eager students, he pointed out the line and asked them again if they wanted to follow him down. One opted in. The other stood with me on the bank, rope in hand, still working on his equations in his head, skeptical of Bob's confidence.

Moments later the lone calculus student and I watched as the two headed down the rapid with Bob out front. Bob laced the line. The other guy, not so much. He got a free cartwheel lesson about halfway down the rapid. But to his credit, he battled out of the hole and made it to the bottom, still in his boat. As for me and the calculus student…we put in below the crux. It would be the only section of the river I would walk that day.

After our second day on Burnt Ranch, Bob and I drove our caravan south, back down I-5, toward our home in Vallejo. Beaming with pride, I no longer had water in my ear or butterflies in my stomach. We were hoping to make it back in time for dinner with my mom so I could tell her all about the trip. I thought to myself, "Fuck you, Tobin. Thanks for the swim lesson. And fuck you too, Willie Nelson. Tonight, kitchen table glory is mine!"

LIFE LESSON

Elders and mentors are like old guide books. You should never judge them by their worn-out covers. The knowledge and experience inside are what counts.

RIVER GUIDE

A BOX CANYON tucked deep within the Trinity Alps of Northern California. Burnt Ranch Gorge is a California classic and a favorite for local paddlers. In their 1984 first edition of California White Water: A Guide to the Rivers, Jim Cassady and Fryar Calhoun described Brunt Ranch Gorge as "one of the best expert runs in California." While the equipment and performance level of kayaking has improved dramatically since the River Shark days, Burnt Ranch is still a notable Class V run worth the attention of nomadic boaters passing through the area.

Pool drop by nature, Burnt Ranch Gorge is an excellent river for advanced kayakers transitioning into expert-level runs. If you love eddy hopping and boofing onto foam piles, you'll fare well on this maze-like run. Most of the rapids require tight maneuvering over or around boulders and hole punching power. You can also expect an occasional brush against the rock walls in some of the more pushy spots.

Depending on how you look at it, one of the best or worst things about Burnt Ranch is that it becomes progressively more difficult as the run continues. This is great in the aspect that it allows you to get warmed up and build into the flow state of mind. However, if you're struggling in the Class IV boulder gardens at the top of the run, you'll need to consider portaging the majority of Class V rapids downstream seriously.

Once in the gorge, the rapids are fast-paced, long and visually stunning. While this sounds gnarly, most of the lines are forgiving at medium to low flows, and most of the Class V rapids can be scouted or portaged. Of course, as the water level rises, the constricted gorge becomes very aggressive and stompy, with retentive holes and massive laterals.

State: **California**
River: **Trinity**
Section: **Burnt Ranch Gorge**
Difficulty: **V**
Gauge: **USGS Trinity River Near Burnt Ranch**
Flow: **500-3,000 cfs**
Distance: **7.75 to 9.25 miles depending on choice of put-in**
Gradient: **50 ft/mi**

Take-Out: Hawkins Bar River Access is located about 90 miles west of Redding, California, on Hwy 299. *40.873139, -123.527874*

Put-In: Cedar Flat River Access is located about 9 miles east of the take-out. From Hawkins Bar, head east on Hwy 299. There will be a large turnout on the right immediately after the Cedar Flat Bridge. *40.790197, -123.439003*

Alternate Put-In: The China Slide Dump is located 8 miles east of Hawkins Bar River Access. Take a hard left on Burnt Ranch Dump Road and follow it down to the river. *40.799638, -123.461059*

CHAPTER 09

OUTTASIGHT

Yankee Jim Canyon, Yellowstone River

"It is the Soldier, not the minister, who has given us freedom of religion.

It is the Soldier, not the reporter, who has given us freedom of the press.

It is the Soldier, not the poet, who has given us freedom of speech.

It is the Soldier, not the campus organizer, who has given us freedom to protest.

It is the Soldier, not the lawyer, who has given us the right to a fair trial.

It is the Soldier, not the politician, who has given us the right to vote.

It is the Soldier who salutes the flag,

Who serves beneath the flag,

And whose coffin is draped by the flag,

Who allows the protester to burn the flag."

— Charles Province

Photo courtesy of Team River Runner

MOST KAYAKERS you meet haven't had their eyes violently blown out of their head, resulting in permanent blindness. But that's precisely what happened to AJ on a fateful day in 2004. Blood, shrapnel, and burned flesh covered his face. AJ's vision was gone, taken from him in a blast, and his life would never be the same.

AJ was on patrol with his Mobile Security Force Detachment in An Najaf Province, Iraq, when enemy forces ambushed them. His life changed the instant their Humvee drove over a bomb buried in the desert road, causing a detonation that disabled the vehicle and trapped the squad in a life or death situation. Tragically, these types of cowardice attacks are common throughout the war-torn Middle East. Since the War on Iraq began in 2003, thousands of U.S. soldiers have died and many more have been wounded by these deadly explosives. AJ was now living the situation that civilians only hear about on the news. Faced with horrific odds, he was forced to choose between 1) staying in the damaged vehicle, 2) getting out to fight for his life, or 3) sprinting to save trapped soldiers in an adjacent burning Humvee. AJ chose option 3, risking his own life to save others.

While dragging a fellow soldier from the burning Humvee, the vehicle exploded, a powerful shockwave of fire, rock, and metal hurling him backward.

Lucky to be alive, he spent the next several months at Balboa Naval Hospital in San Diego, California,

Either die like this or do something about it.

undergoing life-saving and facial reconstructive surgeries. Confined to a hospital bed and now permanently blind, AJ was trapped in a world of visual and emotional darkness.

The next ten years would not be any easier. Suffering from Post-Traumatic Stress Disorder (PTSD), he self-medicated on prescription drugs and alcohol, became obese and depressed, and never left his home without experiencing extreme anxiety. The downward spiral of PTSD and agoraphobia continued for a decade until AJ was finally ready to listen to the warnings of his doctors and mental health advisors: "Either die like this or do something about it."

Unwilling to concede to a pathetic death sentence, AJ decided to do something about it. He summoned the same courage that he used to save the lives of his trapped comrades, but this time he needed to save himself. AJ stopped self-medicating, got out of the house, and began a life-changing journey. Years later, this soldier had won the battle against PTSD, alcoholism, and obesity. He was now healthy and clear-headed. Once an agoraphobic veteran trapped in his house for over a decade, AJ was now traveling the country inspiring others as a respected blind athlete.

And then the river called him....

FROM THE RIVER

A put-in for a river is an unlikely place to meet a blind person. Even more unlikely is seeing a blind person paddle down Class III whitewater. But that's what I witnessed one summer on Yankee Jim Canyon of the Yellowstone River. I had volunteered to be a safety boater for blind veterans participating in an event called Outtasight, a program put on by Team River Runner (TRR). TRR is a non-profit whose mission is to provide veterans and their families an opportunity to find health, healing, community purpose, and new challenges through adventure and adaptive paddlesports.

On this particularly hot and sunny day in July, AJ was one of four blind vets preparing to take on the deep Class III water of Yankee Jim. Other than his dark sunglasses and the orange vest he wore on the water with "Blind Kayaker" in big, bold black print, AJ looked like any kayaker I had ever seen, faded life jacket and all.

Arm in arm, I ushered AJ from the parking lot, down the sandy bank to our boats. There was nothing timid about him. He stood tall and placed every step purposefully. I could tell that he was excited to be on the river and ready to take on the challenges downstream.

If it were me in his booties, I would've been terrified of paddling in the darkness. But once you've survived war, all things are relative.

"It's better that I can't see the rapids," AJ said to me. "I don't get as scared." I admired his honesty and agreed silently.

Before we jumped in our boats, AJ and I went over the communication strategy with our accompanying guide, Nelson. Given AJ's blindness, all communication on the river needed to be auditory and loud. The critical aspects were instructing him on which way to point his boat and timely warnings of hazards downstream like holes, wave trains, rocks, and boils. We also had to give him descriptions about the size of hazards, like "chest-high waves" or "boulder the size of a car." Once we were all on the same page, the three of us headed downstream in a single file line with AJ in the middle.

We practiced our communication as we made our way down the flat water. It was a unique exercise of teamwork on the river. I'd led plenty of new kayakers down rapids before, but taking away the visual elements of kayaking and trying to replace them with auditory cues reminded me of the paddle commands I'd shout while raft guiding. Except, AJ was completely on his own. In a raft, I could shout a command while simultaneously making adjustments to the boat. Left to feel every wave and react immediately to anything that threw him off balance, AJ was both captain and crew of his own craft, kayaking blind, hearing our instructions, but relying on his own senses and quick reactions to make it down safely.

Soon, the canyon narrowed, picking up the pace of the river. We approached the main rapid on Yankee Jim, Boat

Eater.

"First rapid coming up! Big hole and lots of waves! Paddle hard and stay straight!"

The strong current became choppy with lateral waves lapping over the bows of our boats.

"Sweep right! Here comes the hole!"

AJ straightened out his boat and dug in.

"Paddle hard!"

In a brilliant flash of orange and white, AJ entered the white room. He dropped into Boat Eater and was pounded over his chest and shoulders by the hole.

As the wall of whitewater consumed him, his story flashed in front of my eyes: Being ambushed by enemy forces, frantically trying to save his fellow soldiers, the explosion that robbed him of sight, months lying on a hospital bed, a decade of self-medicating to cope with PTSD, the doctors pleading with him to change his life or die alone in his house, and the courage he summoned to survive. Humbled by what I was witnessing, I thought of my own struggles with addiction and the strength it took to get sober. My transformation paled in comparison to what AJ has gone through.

But on that day, in his boat on the Yellowstone River, none of that mattered. There was no hesitation — no timidness. There was just a reaction to the sensation of the river. Just kayaking.

Unwavering, AJ continued to paddle, punched through Boat Eater, and launched off the proceeding peak of the next wave. Stroke after stroke, he laid into the river making small adjustments to lean into the waves.

Despite what his "Blind Kayaker" orange vest labeled him to be, when we came out the other side of Boat Eater, he was a different man in my eyes.

At that moment, AJ wasn't a blind kayaker. He wasn't a blind athlete anymore. He was no longer a wounded vet. Plain and simple, when AJ dropped into that hole and blasted out the other side, he was transformed into one thing and one thing only: a kayaker.

LIFE LESSON

Bravery doesn't always mean running big rapids or fighting in a war. Sometimes the most courageous thing a person can do is decide to change the path they are on and commit to a better life.

RIVER GUIDE

YANKEE JIM CANYON is one of only two whitewater
stretches on the iconic Yellowstone River. Because of
its proximity to the northern entrance of Yellowstone
National Park, Yankee Jim probably floats more
international tourists than any other stretch of water in
the country. The Park typically accommodates around 4
million visitors each year, many of whom are eager for a
whitewater adventure. Yankee Jim provides the perfect
backdrop for these would-be paddlers with stunning
scenery, wildlife, exciting rapids, and deep waters.

Most of Yankee Jim is lined with smooth grey boulders,
held in place by the woody, arid flora along the bank of
the Yellowstone River. Rocky Mountain Junipers, with
their gnarled trunks and flaky brown bark, display their
complex roots to travelers looking outward from the
river. The juniper's dense sage canopies provide cover
for darting birds and welcome shade for boaters taking a
break. During spring runoff, sediment from surrounding

Ford Smith and Sam Freihofer in Boat Eater by William Freihofer tributaries makes the water resemble chocolate milk. As flows subside from spring to fall, the water color changes from a deep dark grey to a vibrant turquoise on sunny days. In between the walls of the canyon, where most of the severe rapids roar, the dark grey cliffs are always reflected in the current below, creating a spooky feeling of a bottomless pit.

Water volume from spring to fall changes dramatically. During spring runoff, the river can see swollen flows exceeding 20,000 cfs. However, late fall hovers around only one grand. Yankee Jim is a prominent spot for whitewater paddlers during the spring and summer months. But once the flows drop below 5,000 cfs, the fishermen drop their oars and flock to cast for browns, rainbows, and the threatened Yellowstone cutthroat trout. Whether you're rowing an oar-rig casting for lunkers, or you're a kayaker looking for holes to punch, Yankee Jim delivers at all levels. But be warned. Casualties are an annual occurrence. Its deep waters, swirling eddy lines, and continuous current have been known to pull swimmers into the dark abyss for good.

State: Montana
River: Yellowstone River
Section: Yankee Jim Canyon
Difficulty: III-IV
Gauge: USGS Yellowstone River at Corwin Springs MT
Flow: 1,000 - 25,000 cfs
Distance: 4.25 miles
Gradient: 13 ft/mi

Take-Out: Carbella Campground is located 17 miles north of Gardiner, Montana, on Hwy 89. Turn left onto Tom Miner Creek Rd., hang an immediate right down the dirt road to the big parking lot and boat ramp. *45.212484, -110.900540*

Put-In: Yankee Jim Picnic Area is 3.8 miles south of the take-out and 13 miles north of Gardiner between the river and Hwy 89. *45.168237, -110.854865*

CHAPTER 10

LUCKY TO BE ALIVE

Quake Lake, Madison River

"Luck is what you have left after you give 100 percent."
— Langston Coleman

THERE ARE moments in every person's life when letting your guard down at the wrong time can have serious consequences. When complacency can change your trajectory entirely. The aftermath so significant that we must fight with everything we have to get our lives back on track. Sometimes our best isn't good enough, and luck is the deciding factor. In a dynamic and hazardous environment like a Class V river, staying focused is critical.

Complacency is sneaky. In my experience, carelessness usually creeps in near the end of a hard run when I'm fatigued or overconfident in familiar territory. A false sense of security sets in, which can have serious consequences. This has happened to me more times than I'd like to admit. Perhaps it's toward the end of a difficult run when all the "hard" rapids are behind me, but a sticky little hole gives me an unexpected smackdown. Or maybe I'm playboating a familiar run at high water when a strong eddy line causes me to whiff a few rolls and go for a swim. Sometimes the consequences are extreme, lost boat or

Joe Vincent and Connor Fitzgerald in Quake by Kevin Kennedy

injury, other times it's just a shot to the ego. Regardless of the outcome, it was over-confidence that put me there in the first place. Now the energy required to correct the situation is dramatically more than what it would have taken if I'd just stayed focused. But instead, I try to course correct out of the predicament that I put myself in by being sloppy.

If I hadn't been careless, to begin with, everything would have gone to plan. But instead, a tremendous amount of effort is required to rectify the situation. In urgent cases, my best shot may not be good enough and I'm unable to overcome the obstacles in front of me. That idea goes against the "can do" optimistic attitude many people believe in, but it's the reality. The cold hard truth is that sometimes a person may face overwhelming hurdles that cannot be beaten, regardless of their attitude or effort. People die on the river every year. Sometimes it was because of complacency, more often it's because they were overwhelmed by the elements. That's why it is critical to remain vigilant at all times and use good judgment.

So where does luck come into play with all of this doom and gloom? Luck is hard to define. Think of it as a force outside of our control, brought by chance rather than effort. It can be considered a higher power unbiased toward outcomes but somehow influencing them. I don't think it's a god waving a finger at the right time (religious people have been dying for thousands of years, regardless of how much they pray or who they pray to). It's not karma catching up to people, either (in a plane crash, a good person will die just like a bad person). Luck is the blind chance that is beyond understanding or control and should never be relied upon.

Still, there are times when we need it in order to survive. But we also need to give an extreme effort. That's why preparation and discipline are critical. A vigorous and determined fight for our lives will increase our chances for survival. By giving 100 percent, we're giving ourselves a fighting chance for luck to do the rest. Depending on the challenge, this combination of battle and luck may be the key to success or failure. But without one or the other, failure is inevitable. Sometimes we need both luck and effort. We can't rely on luck to pull us out of the river. We must swim to shore. Which means we must first learn to swim, and then apply the skills at the right time. If we don't know how to swim, all the luck in the world won't get us out of the water. But if we're unlucky and get knocked unconscious by the river rocks while swimming, the skill and effort are useless. There are crucial moments when we need both effort and luck. In these moments of life or death, we must be able to give 100 percent of ourselves if we want to paddle another day.

If we become complacent at the wrong time, there may be consequences. Sometimes they are so severe that it changes everything in an instant. We go from enjoying life to fighting for it. Maybe the fight is too difficult to overcome. Or perhaps luck intervenes to give us a second chance. Focus and preparation are critical to helping us avoid these types of situations. And with a little bit of luck, maybe we won't get stuck there in the first place.

FROM THE RIVER

Everything went fine on the first run down Quake that afternoon. I had taken the same line down S-turn I'd done a dozen times before. Although the move is always tricky, I always ran it clean. The second run that day was a different story.

I led our group down the upper section of continuous Class IV. As we had done the prior run, I peeled into the eddy just about S-turn to catch my breath and regroup. But this time, my crew continued past me without eddying out. No big deal, I thought, as I pulled out of the eddy still feeling out of breath from the upper section.

I knew I was about 10 feet out of position from my usual line as I floated toward the first hole. In a moment of poor judgement, I had no sense of urgency to get back on track. I figured I would just boof the top hole, get back on my normal line, and rally the rest of the long rapid. I put in a few medium effort strokes and boofed. My lackadaisical paddling resulted in an immediate beatdown. Because I had always focused on sticking to my left line and avoiding this hazard, I had never realized how wide and sticky the hole was. So now I was getting violently recirculated on the entry hole of a quarter-mile-long Class V rapid.

I tried every evasive maneuver I could to get out of the nasty hydraulic. Moves I'd mastered over the years while practicing on more forgiving hazards for moments just like this: Side surf and breathe, assess the hole and possible exits, flip around to side surf both directions while trying to claw out, multiple rolls while trying to grab the undercurrent. It all happens in split-seconds, but with a calm head and the right hole, these techniques help a paddler get out of tricky spots. But this hole was different, and it wasn't letting me go. Its deep angle and horseshoe shape pushes boats down and center with a powerful force that sends kayaks cartwheeling.

I was doing everything I could to get out of this hole and

keep breathing, but I quickly ran out of options, as well as air and energy. I knew I'd need both if I was going to get out of its grasp. I also knew I wasn't getting out of that hole in my kayak. The boat's buoyancy was like a magnet to the hydraulic pressure. I had to swim out. I wasn't in a state of panic or fear when I made this fateful decision. I was calm, present, and accepted the fact that I might need to swim every inch of S-turn before I would be able to reach an eddy. I knew the rapid well and what I needed to do.

"Swim left as hard and as long as it takes," I thought.

Fully committed, I took a deep breath, let go of my paddle, and pulled my skirt.

The next minute tested every ounce of my survival instincts in a way I have never experienced before. I felt the accelerating surge as the current ripped me from my boat. My body was rag-dolled by the river as I tumbled violently through holes and was dragged over rock ledges. By the time I came up for air, I'd already been underwater for close to 40 yards. Committed to my original plan, I rolled over, and with a slight upstream angle, swam left as hard as I possibly could.

"Stick to the plan. You'll grab one of these little eddies sooner or later," I thought to myself while swimming as hard as I could and desperately scanning the rocks on the left bank for a suitable eddy.

I found one eventually. But it was barely the size of my torso, not large enough to protect me from the current. I struggled to grip a large algae-covered rock on the river's edge as tightly as I could. But the drag on my lower body was too strong. I watched as my fingernails clawed scratches on the rock as the river pulled me by my legs back into the powerful rapids.

Now back in the main current, I continued to swim left as hard as I could when my hip hit a rock underwater and suddenly spun me face-first downstream. A head-on collision with a rock on a river like this could be fatal. Without your feet in front of you to kick off rocks, a swimmer is completely exposed and could easily get knocked unconscious. I knew I was in trouble. Before I was able to spin back around or even put my hands over my face, I was flushed through a narrow slot. Then SMACK! My face pounded the bottom of the river. I could feel my front teeth crumble and saw a bright flash of light.

The grave reality of the situation set in as my lifejacket floated me to the surface.

"This is serious! You need to get out of the river NOW!" I thought to myself as I came back up for air, spitting out chunks of my shattered teeth while desperately trying to breathe.

The river would not let up. At this point, my head was foggy from the collision, and I barely had enough energy to keep my feet downstream. Waves continued to wash over my face, obstructing my breathing and visibility.

"This is what it's like to flush drown." The words raced through my mind as I felt empathy for all of the paddlers I had heard of drowning over the years. Relentlessly, the river swept me under the surface again and slammed my body into rock after rock.

But I wasn't done fighting.

"I'm not dying on this river! I'm not fucking dying today!"

A surge of adrenaline kicked in and I pulled myself to the surface just in time to see another big horizon line right in front of my feet. I took a huge deep breath and was swept over the ledge.

I disappeared for another 20 yards underwater. When I came up, things got worse. My right leg slipped between a pile of rocks on the riverbed, causing a foot entrapment just below the knee — an absolute worst-case scenario on any river. With my leg locked into place by my ankle and shinbone, the entire weight of the river washed over my back and folded me over at the waist, face down below the surface. As the pain of my knee hyperextending began, I felt my entire right leg cramp up to protect it from snapping in place. I don't know where it came from, but instinctively, I mustered the strength to position myself in a way that allowed me to place my free left leg on top of one of the rocks trapping me. I got my head above water and took a deep breath. I pushed straight up with my left leg while I yanked my trapped limb as hard as I could. It worked. I felt my right leg squeeze out from between the rocks that had locked it in place. I was free, and once again flowing in the swift current.

By now I was physically and mentally running on fumes. I knew I was through the crux of the rapid, but another 200 yards of continuous Class IV hole punching and submerged tree trunks were in store if I didn't get out now. There was no way I could survive another beating like that. At this point, I was desperately fighting for my life. I saw a pile of rocks breaking the surface of the water close to the left bank. There had to be an eddy behind it that would offer some reprieve from the rapids. I swam toward the pile and threw myself on top of them. The river washed me up and around, planting me in an eddy just big enough for my entire body. I had made it. My swim was over and I was alive.

Emotions swept over me. I began to whimper in the eddy as tears of relief and joy flooded my eyes. I could breathe. I was alive. I had made it out. Once my crew arrived and helped me out of the river, I assessed my physical state. My fingernails were bleeding from clawing at the rocks. Three of my front teeth were broken into pieces from my face-first collision with the river bed. My chin bled from a deep laceration, and my jaw felt like it was broken. Both of my legs were bruised and bleeding from being dragged over so many rocks. And my right knee felt likeI had torn ligaments and tendons from the foot entrapment. As I laid broken in the eddy, none of the physical pain and injury mattered to me. I was alive. Somehow, I managed to survive.

There is a part of me, my ego mainly, that wants to believe that it was a culmination of knowledge and skill that kept me from drowning; that I had saved my own life by calling upon 35 years of river experience. A part of me can't let go of the sense of control and pride that I had somehow prepared myself to survive those types of situations. Perhaps it's that ego and pride that allowed my overconfidence in the first place — the same complacent attitude that got me stuck in the hole at the top of S-turn and almost killed me.

There's no doubt that all the preparation and my will to survive gave me a fighting chance. I wouldn't have walked off the river that day without it. But even though I swam and fought as hard as I could, it was luck that kept me alive.

When I was spun around and flushed head first down the slot, I was lucky that I wasn't knocked unconscious. I got lucky that I had time to spit out my teeth and take a deep breath before I was flushed into one of the biggest holes. When my leg got trapped between two rocks, I was lucky that I had enough leverage with my other leg to pull myself free before my leg broke. Lastly, I got lucky that the pile of rocks I was hoping would have an eddy behind them wasn't a sieve that would have trapped me for good.

I didn't save myself. Luck saved me. But I did give myself a fighting chance. I gave 100 percent, and luck was all that remained. Without my hard work, I wouldn't be here. Without luck, I wouldn't be here. I needed them both.

RIVER GUIDE

IN THE SUMMER OF '59, my father-in-law and his family enjoyed an idyllic Montana weekend. They had loaded the family station wagon and made the beautiful drive from Great Falls to camp and fish along the pristine Madison River — a gentle trout-filled stream, which meandered through a pine forest. At the conclusion of their weekend, they packed up the station wagon, leaving the peaceful campsite and river in the rearview mirror.

All of that natural serenity would be wiped out nearly one week later.

Close to midnight on August 17, 1959, in pitch-black darkness, a 7.2 magnitude earthquake shook southwest Montana and surrounding areas. Its epicenter was within the Madison Canyon, just west of Yellowstone National Park. Powerful shock waves caused a massive landslide

Dave Schroeder in S-turn by Nick Gottlieb

which completely blocked the flow of the Madison River with 50 million cubic yards of rock, mud, and trees. Homes in the area toppled. Roads were torn apart. New geysers appeared in Yellowstone overnight. And the campsite my father-in-law enjoyed as a child was buried in an instant by the landslide, its debris killing 28 sleeping campers.

As a result of the earthquake and dammed river, the Army Corp of Engineers began a massive project to free the Madison River from the newly formed and quickly rising, Earthquake Lake. They blasted and bulldozed a channel to allow the river to flow once again. Forged of sharp jagged rock and splintered pine tree trunks, this channel of water is what kayakers now refer to as "Quake Lake."

Putting in at Quake is eerie. Freestanding dead trees sticking out of the water act as a warning for all who dare approach the horizon line where peaceful Earthquake Lake becomes the hazardous whitewater section of Quake. Weathered grey by the elements, the trees look like ghostly tombstones for the 28 campers killed in the landslide of '59.

Once you cross the threshold of the lake to the river, there is no turning back. The action starts immediately and doesn't end until you take out at the bottom. The consistent gradient of the upper section offers nonstop Class IV boofing and hole punching. Quake's steep riverbed is layered with sharp rocks, sticky river-wide holes, powerful currents, scattered wood, and tight sieves. The rocks can easily injure an upside-down paddler, flush-drown a swimmer, or trap a leg at any moment.

Midway down the run is a large eddy on river left which provides the opportunity to regroup or hop out and scout S-turn. A quarter-mile-long Class V rapid, S-turn encompasses every hazard imaginable and has claimed the life of kayakers in the past. A strong local paddler flush-drowned here in 2008 while the river was cranking above 3,000 cfs. Even with adequate safety precautions, the swim proved fatal. My accident occurred at a third of that flow, which was still powerful enough to send me to the hospital.

Below S-turn, Quake resumes its Class IV boogie water for another hundred yards before tinkering out to Class III currents. At this point, look for any good eddy on the right to pull out. Once you're out of the river, you have a decision to make: Call it a day or run multiple laps. Whatever you decide, stay focused, have fun, and be safe.

State: **Montana**
River: **Madison**
Section: **Quake Lake**
Difficulty: **V**
Gauge: **UGSG Madison River below Hebgen Lake**
Flow: **900-3,000 cfs**
Distance: **1 mile**
Gradient: **160 ft/mi**

Take-Out: Grab an eddy anywhere after the Class III boogie water ends. Hike or hitch back to the top. *44.827386, -111.439566*

Put-In: From Ennis, Montana, head south on Hwy 287 for 44 miles to the Quake Lake Visitors Center. Across the highway from the visitors center is a large dirt turnout. There is a road to the right that goes down to the lake. *44.830222, -111.423429*

OUT LIVING IT

Moccasin to West Glacier, Middle Fork of the Flathead

"We have this obligation to go out and live as fully as possible."

— **Brad Ludden,** Founder of First Descents

TRACTOR WALKED to his boat, carefully navigating the river rock beneath his Crocs sandals. He braced with his paddle as he sat down on top of his red kayak to begin unstrapping his prosthetic.

"Lewinsky, would you please hold my leg?" asked Tractor as he handed me his state-of-the-art robotic limb.

He wouldn't need it in his kayak anyway. Once Tractor was in his boat, you'd never know his right leg ended above his knee. The only people on the river that day who knew about Tractor's amputated leg were the safety volunteers, like me, and the other dozen First Descents participants, each with their own stories of surviving childhood cancer, some with visible signs, others without. And all of us sported goofy nicknames like "Lewinsky," "Tractor," "Pinky," "The Brain," or whatever random moniker we were given at the beginning of the week.

Using nature as a metaphor for navigating life — just as I'm trying to do with kayaking — First Descents provides life-changing, outdoor adventures for young adults impacted by cancer. I was fortunate to volunteer as a safety boater with the organization for many summers in Montana, Colorado, and Washington. I was unfortunate to be given the nickname "Lewinsky." "Tractor" sounds way cooler. Although we didn't get to pick our nicknames (you never do), Tractor's suited him well — and not just because of his mechanical limb. He was a big burly dude. Other than his missing extremity, you'd be surprised that he ever had cancer as a child.

The night before our first river trip, we sat around the campfire singing Tractor's hit single, "Iso Track 2500." It was a song he had written and put to guitar, about the experience of losing his leg to cancer. Tractor named it after the rowing machine he used to train for his week-long kayaking adventure with First Descents. He played his guitar and sang "Iso Track 2500" like a guy with a passion for life and loud rock music. His energy pulled us all into the lyrics. Before we knew it, we were all singing as loud as we could, too.

"I-sooo-track-twenty-fiiive-huun-dred! I-sooo-track-twenty-fiiive-huun-dred!"

Tractor's heavy guitar chords along with our booming voices filled the big Montana night sky. The lyrics were like a battle cry for a group of triumphant warriors who had fought a personal war. A team of survivorsf who fought cancer at an age when they should have been out running and playing with other kids. Instead, they spent summers in hospital rooms, missed their proms, and had years taken from them and their families.

While each participant had their own unique story of battling cancer and came from different parts of the country, they had all assembled that week in Montana with one common goal — to learn how to whitewater kayak. If they could survive cancer, surely they could handle a week on the river. For them, the week would be a lesson in paddling. For me, the week would be a lesson in what resilience truly means.

FROM THE RIVER

Although we made it clear that a swim-fest was imminent, there was no discouraging these brave kayakers. The group decision had been made to run the Class III- stretch, Moccasin to West Glacier. The alternative would be the more mellow II+ upstream, Bear Creek to Paola. It was no surprise that they chose the more challenging section. These people beat cancer, they weren't scared of a river. They would rather risk swimming on the hard stuff than float the easy stuff. How could anyone argue with that?

The next morning as we set off for the river, some people were a little nervous and others were a lot nervous. It's one thing to be brave from the couch the night before, but it's completely different when you're standing on the bank looking at the swift current. Before the group put on, we had our typical safety meeting to discuss what lay ahead. There was lots of talk about staying together in the fast-moving current, rapids we'd scout, lunch plans, and group concerns. As a safety boater, your job is simple — guide people down rapids, smile, help swimmers, and give lots of high fives. It's easy to forget that the people you're guiding can be tense, scared, and hesitant. This was the case with several paddlers that morning.

To help ease the tension, we added something extra to that morning's safety meeting. Another camp volunteer, known as "The Brain," stepped up to give an epic pep talk.

A world-class slalom kayaker and former member of the U.S. National Team, The Brain knew how to be mentally tough under pressure. He shared a past experience of keeping a cool head as he competed for a spot on the national squad. With one run left to secure a spot on the team, he was sitting in the calm water above the slalom course feeling all the pressure in the world. But instead of focusing on finishing with a qualifying time downstream, he decided to focus on the one thing he could control immediately — his first stroke out of the gate. He concentrated on the initial horizon line that would lead into the first drop of the course. On that horizon line was a small curling wave. And off that curling wave sprung a single drop of water. In that big moment, The Brain set his sights on getting to that one tiny drop of water. Instead of taking on the enormity of the situation, he remained completely present and focused on one task.

Our group stood at the put-in listening to The Brain's pep talk about staying calm and present. We could all relate to this message in one way or another. But for

> **It's one thing to be brave from the couch the night before, but it's completely different when you're standing on the bank looking at the swift current.**

many of the First Descents participants, the message was received on a deeper level. These were people who had experienced times when all they had was the present tense. Cancer treatments of various sorts had put their lives on hold. There was no guarantee of tomorrow. If they could survive those traumatic life events, Moccasin to West Glacier would be a cinch.

The Brain's pep talk did the trick. As we pushed off the bank, the group was excited and happy to be on the river again. Although it was a challenging run for the team, their grit and resilience persevered. We worked our way downstream as a group, rapid after rapid, and eddy after eddy. And we did so with smiles, laughs, and more swims than we could count.

LIFE LESSON

Give your internal strength a chance to muster by taking a moment to connect with the present.

RIVER GUIDE

FROM THE RIVER // OUT LIVING IT

ONE FLOAT DOWN the Middle Fork of the Flathead and you'll understand why it's designated as a National Wild & Scenic River. Its deep waters cut a lush valley between Glacier National Park on river-right and the Bob Marshall Wilderness on river-left. The National Wild and Scenic Rivers System was created by the Wild and Scenic Rivers Act of 1968, enacted by the U.S. Congress to "preserve certain rivers with outstanding natural, cultural, and recreational values in a free-flowing condition for the enjoyment of present and future generations." With year-round visitors fishing, rafting, hiking, and photographing the river, it's no wonder the local community rallied in 1976 to get the river on the list.

The stretch between Moccasin and West Glacier is a great spot for beginner kayakers to get a taste of paddling in a big river. With relatively high flows, this wide streambed packs a lot of action. Pool-drop by character, the river gives paddlers a chance to relax and enjoy the scenery between the spread-out Class II-III rapids. Most of the rapids are straight-forward with crashing wave trains, hole punching, and occasional rock dodging. But due to the high volume and deep water, unpredictable boils and swirling eddy lines also exist — features that make prime swim conditions for paddlers still developing their fundamentals.

As you approach the end of the run, you'll pass under the beautiful Belton Bridge. This historic river crossing served as the western entrance to Glacier National Park from 1920-1938. Now its main purpose is a hang-out spot for local bridge jumpers and tourists. On our day on the water with First Descents, Tractor sent it off Belton Bridge one-legged style. When he came to the surface, there were cheers and chants of "Iso Track 2500!"

State: **Montana**
River: **Middle Fork of the Flathead**
Section: **Lower Stretch, Moccasin to West Glacier**
Difficulty: **III-**
Gauge: **USGS MF Flathead near West Glacier MT**
Flow: **1,000-12,000 cfs**
Distance: **7 miles**
Gradient: **18 ft/mi**

Take-Out: West Glacier River Access is located about 1.5 miles from downtown West Glacier, Montana. From Hwy 2, go left on Going to the Sun Rd, then another left on River Bend Dr, turn right at the T in front of the condos to stay on River Bend Dr. About a half-mile down the road, the entrance to the take-out will be on the right. Alternate take-outs upstream are Belton Bridge and Going to the Sun Road Bridge, both are close proximity to West Glacier. *48.504975, -113.993975*

Put-In: Moccasin Creek River Access is located about 7.5 miles east of West Glacier. From Going to the Sun Rd, head left on Hwy 2. The driveway to Moccasin Creek will be on your left. *48.480513, -113.847432*

CHAPTER 12

OBSTACLES BECOME OPPORTUNITIES

Mad Mile, Gallatin River

"Growth begins when we begin to accept our own weakness."

— **Jean Vanier**

HONEST SELF-REFLECTION IS DIFFICULT. That's one of the reasons Improving our lives can be challenging. First, we have to look at our current situation, decide what we want to do differently, and then make the change happen. Most of us don't take the time for self-examination. And when we do, the ability to make an honest assessment is challenging. We have biases and beliefs that hold us back from gathering an objective inventory. Even if we're able to take accurate stock, deciding on the next course of action toward self-improvement is hard. Perhaps we set too lofty a goal, so we conclude that it's out of reach. Or maybe the effort is too daunting, so we slide back onto the couch. It could be that we don't know how to achieve the goal and we aren't willing to seek out guidance. Whatever the reasons, if we want to make our lives better, overcoming these barriers is necessary.

For kayakers, the river can be a place for honest self-reflection. Because the river is objective by nature,

Neil Seifert on The Whale by Forest Ledger

it provides immediate feedback. There's no bias on the water. No combat roll? Guess what? You're swimming. Screwed up your boof stroke? Here comes the rodeo. Forgot your helmet again? Thanks for running shuttle. If we pay attention to the river, we'll learn a lot about ourselves and what to do about it. Don't want to swim? Practice your roll. Getting stuck in too many holes? Improve your boof. Keep forgetting gear? Stop smoking so much weed. You get good-old honest feedback from the mouth of the river itself.

With the river's help, we can acknowledge our abilities and take the next step toward improvement. But the river doesn't only expose our weaknesses; it also provides us with opportunities to develop our strengths. Every obstacle on the river can be a feature for building new skills. That combat roll problem? Practice your roll in the Class II current or gentle eddy lines between drops. Boof still suck? Send it off every little rock and wave you see. Helmet missing again? Duct tape that damn thing to your head! Before you know it, you'll have made significant improvements to your boating by leveraging the obstacles in the river as opportunities to develop.

FROM THE RIVER

When I die, fold some of my ashes in an origami kayak and send me down the beautiful Gallatin River one last time. If I'm lucky, I'll be reincarnated as a merganser and paddle this stretch in my next life, too.

Why do I love the Gallatin so much? The Gally is like a second home that welcomes you back with open arms anytime you stop by. It's a hospitable river offering just about everything a kayaker could ask for. It's the type of river a person can embrace and decide what kind of experience they want to have. I've spent countless hours on the Gallatin developing my strengths as a kayaker, training incessantly, focused solely on improving my paddling. I've also spent equal time just relaxing and enjoying the water, with no agenda at all. Regardless of what drew me to the river that day, the Gallatin always delivered.

Having a river that you can hone your craft on can be both a blessing and a curse for someone like me. One of my mistakes was I used the river as an escape from reality and responsibility. I wasn't just running to the river, I was also running from my responsibilities off the water. So I threw myself into paddling with only one selfish goal: get better at all costs. It was no longer about enjoying the river or people I paddled with. In fact, many times I would head out by myself for solo missions. I put pressure on myself to improve and resented anyone or anything that stood between me and paddling. I didn't have time to wait for people's schedules to clear up so they could paddle with me. I didn't care about the social aspect of paddling so much as I did the competitive side. I just wanted to be the "best" paddler I could be.

Without realizing it, my intense drive eventually dissolved the fun I once had on the water. This type of obsessive behavior, on the river and in other areas of my life, eventually led to burnout and crash. At this point, I had to step away from the river and face the harsh reality — that my selfish pursuits had alienated me from the people I cared for most and my life had become unmanageable. Just like the river exposes a kayaker's weaknesses, life had begun to reveal my personal shortcomings.

I hung up my boat for over a year to focus on more critical areas of my life. (Yes, there are more important things than adventure.) When I got back to a good place in my personal life, I decided to head back to the Gallatin with a new perspective of humility and gratitude. I had a new definition of what it meant to be a solid kayaker — balanced with other priorities in my life. My sense of self-worth had broadened beyond just running Class V on the weekends. I reinvested quality time with my loved ones on and off the water. No more solo missions to isolate and escape. Instead, I looked forward to the camaraderie that kayaking brings just as much as the excitement. I also came to appreciate the importance of staying home with my wife on the weekends to run errands and have a date night. As a result, our marriage grew stronger. As I found balance and contentment off the river, I also found joy in paddling again. Every eddy line, every ripple of water, and every salmonfly hatch presented new opportunities for gratitude —opportunities I had missed when I was selfishly focused on being the "best" paddler I could be.

LIFE LESSON

To improve our situation, we have to be honest and objective with ourselves. Only when we have accepted our weaknesses, can we commit to taking the necessary steps for change.

RIVER GUIDE

Travis Lehman in House Rock by Bob Booth

A WORLD-CLASS RIVER in its own right, the Gallatin River Canyon offers excellent access, spectacular scenery, abundant wildlife, and diverse recreation opportunities. A free-flowing river with headwaters meandering out of Yellowstone National Park, the "Gally" is a hub for area fishermen, climbers, hikers, and of course, paddlers. Since it's only 30 minutes outside of Bozeman, Montana, Gally laps before or after work are a common pastime for locals.

The Gallatin is good at virtually any flow from early spring to late fall, with new features coming into play as water levels ebb and flow throughout the year. This variety provides local paddlers with a completely different experience during spring runoff compared to summer flows.

At peak runoff, the two-mile stretch from Lava to

Storm Castle is thrilling for all ability levels. The action is virtually non-stop as you navigate crashing waves and beefy holes. House Rock, which can be scouted from the road, is an intimidating Class IV drop with a successive boulder garden that has caused multiple drownings and countless swims. Immediately following the boulder garden is the Mad Mile, a non-stop wave train with retentive holes and few eddies.

Once the runoff ends, the character of the Gallatin mellows to a chill Class III. Boulders that line the riverbed start to reveal themselves and offer ample play spots for surfing, splats, and boofs. This is the perfect level for working on fundamentals and mastering new skills. It's also during summer flows that beginner and intermediate kayakers decide to challenge themselves on this section. This provides more advanced boaters the opportunity to practice philanthropy by helping others learn — an often overlooked, but always rewarding part of our sport.

State: **Montana**
River: **Gallatin River**
Section: **Lava to Storm Castle**
Difficulty: **III-IV**
Gauge: **USGS Gallatin River near Gallatin Gateway**
Flow: **500-6,000 cfs (or higher if you can get it!)**
Distance: **1 miles**
Gradient: **130 ft/mi**

Take-Out: Hellroaring River Access (also referred to as Storm Castle) is located 13 miles south of Gallatin Gateway, Montana, on Hwy 191. This well-maintained dirt river access is on the left as you head south from Gateway. It's easy to miss, so keep your eye open for it. *45.428815, -111.232758*

Put-In: Lava Lake Turnout is located upstream about 2 miles from the take-out. You'll get plenty of road scouting in as you drive. Once you cross the bridge, immediately pull into the large turnout on the right. *45.407124, -111.225088*

CHAPTER 13

SHOW ME THE LINE
Swinging Bridge, Kootenai River

"You are not IN the universe, you ARE the universe, an intrinsic part of it. Ultimately you are not a person, but a focal point where the universe is becoming conscious of itself. What an amazing miracle."

— **Eckhart Tolle**

THERE IS AN ART and a science to reading water. An experienced kayaker knows that the river will show them the line, not the other way around. The river makes the rules, and it is up to us, as voyagers on its water, to follow them. Even the strongest paddler cannot go where the river will not allow. Sure, you can ferry across a powerful current or slam into a micro-eddy. But no one can paddle back up a 30-foot waterfall or fit through a strainer smaller than their boat. Simply put, the river provides directions that we as kayakers must follow. It's up to us to read its waters and determine which way the river wants us to go.

Reading water can be a challenge for both beginner and advanced kayakers. I've stood on banks with paddlers of all abilities and seen them struggle to "see the line" until someone shows them. Watching someone run a rapid to see the line versus reading water to choose your own route are very different things. When a paddler reads water, they ask the river to show them the way. This intimate moment between kayaker and river requires deep observation and self-reflection. By asking this of the river, you connect with it by practicing humility and understanding. This special connection is lost when a paddler waits for a demonstration by a fellow boater.

FROM THE RIVER

The Kootenai River had been on my to-do list ever since I picked up a copy of *Montana Surf* by Nick Turner, Matt Wilson, and Russ Fry, back in the spring of 2005. It wasn't until fall 2017 that I finally made my way up there with my dad and a group of friends. The Kootenai is a big, stompy high water run. Being my first time down, I wanted to make sure I stuck to the conservative lines and stayed in my boat. Given the size of the rapids, boat scouting was difficult. Luckily a few guys in our group were familiar with the rapids, so they provided general beta like, "Stay right of the massive hole in the middle." I was content to let my trusted teammates show me the lines.

About halfway down the run, we had our first swimmer. Because of the swift current and boiling eddy walls, it took a three-person effort to get him and his boat to shore just before dropping over the next horizon. As our swimmer drained his boat, we stood on river right scouting the next blind drop. Because the river is so wide and steep in this section, we weren't able to get good eyes on anything other than the first move. Two of us tried to billy-goat along the right bank and could glimpse the river-left line. It looked gnarly, and I wasn't confident that I would be able to make the moves. So in a moment of humility, I asked the river to show me the line that would work best for me. The river answered. On the opposite bank above the rapid, stood a giant boulder that seemed to tower over the river. If I could ferry across the powerful current, eddy out, and climb the rock, I'd have the best view of both river-left and river-right. I let the team know that I wasn't comfortable with river left and that I planned on ferrying across to see what river-right had in store. It would take more time and effort, but I knew it was the right thing to do.

Once atop the boulder I could see the right line was the best option — still big and bouncy, but clean. So I ferried back across, described the line to my guys, and in a moment of pride, led the group down the super fun right side. Once we were all below the rapid, I was able to assess the big picture and see that the right line was definitely the best option. I had made the correct decision to take time to scout the rapid and choose the line with which I felt most comfortable. I asked the river to show me the line, and it did. At that moment, my connection to the water grew stronger and my confidence solidified for the rest of the trip.

LIFE LESSON

Practicing humility keeps us honest with ourselves. Take an extra moment to gain more perspective on a situation before you act.

RIVER GUIDE

MADE FAMOUS by the 1994 adventure thriller starring
Meryl Streep, The River Wild, the big water of the
Kootenai River flows south from British Columbia into
Montana through the town of Libby. Seventeen miles
upstream of Libby stands the 422-foot-tall Libby Dam,
which provides power to eight states: Montana, Idaho,
Washington, Wyoming, California, Utah, Oregon, and
Nevada. The controlled release of massive flows from the
hydro-power dam provides area kayakers with predictable
and high water excitement. A typical year will see water
levels vary from 2,000 cfs to 30,000 cfs. The sweet spot for
paddlers is the 6,000 cfs to 12,000 cfs range, which offers
colossal wave trains, powerful holes, swirling Class IV-V
rapids, boiling eddy lines, and waterfalls.

The action starts 12 miles west of Libby at Kootenai
Falls; the put-in for this big-water run. Many paddlers
are drawn to this run just because of this waterfall. As

Joe Booth on the Kootenai by Bob Booth

beautiful as it is intimidating, Kootenai Falls is a massive river-wide, 25-foot ledge drop. On any given weekend, you can expect bounds of tourists admiring the falls and questioning the sanity of kayakers willing to run the drop. There are various lines depending on the flow, but most people stick to channels on river left. Choose your line carefully and set ample safety. This is not a plop-and-drop waterfall in and out of calm eddies. Kootenai Falls is extremely wide, so it's easy to lose your line from above. Immediately below the falls are ledge holes that will beat you down if you aren't ready (and sometimes even when you are).

Whether you choose to run Kootenai Falls or not, there is ample big-water Class IV to be had. Below the falls the river splits into two wide channels, with stompy whitewater to the right and a hidden 12-foot waterfall to the left. Chances are you'll be running multiple laps, so you'll get the chance to run both options if the flows are right.

There are only about seven notable rapids on the Kootenai. Although it's a relatively short run and pool-drop in nature, the high flow and steady current tie it all together quickly. Keep an eye on your fellow paddlers and make an urgent attempt to get to swimmers and floating gear out of the river.

State: **Montana**
River: **Kootenai**
Section: **Swinging Bridge**
Difficulty: **IV-V**
Flow: **6,000-12,000 cfs**
Gauge: **USGS Kootenai River bl Libby Dam nr Libby MT**

Distance: **1.2 miles**
Gradient: **100 ft/mi**

Take-Out: 1 mile west of the put-in is a large turnout on the south side of the highway. From the river, you'll see a large sandbar on the left. Hike your boats up the hill, picking up any trash you see along the way. *48.447550, -115.783822*

Put-In: 12 miles west of Libby, Montana, at Kootenai Falls. Look for the large turnout parking lot on the north side of the Hwy 2. Hike your boat down the hill, over the railroad track, and up to the falls. *48.454782, -115.764001*

CHAPTER 14

KEEP COMING BACK

Hells Canyon, Boulder River

"I decided to abandon the trip, with then and there immediate determination, as soon as a new outfit could be secured, to return and complete our journey to the Gulf."

— Robert Brewster Stanton
Stanton's railroad survey party was the second crew to run the Grand Canyon in 1889

HAVE YOU EVER laid awake at night thinking about an incomplete task or goal? Maybe you toss and turn in bed analyzing a run that you weren't able to complete? Perhaps you were disappointed by a swim you had on the river that day. Or by all the rapids you portaged. Or maybe you decided to abandon the run entirely and hike off the river. Regardless of what caused you to come up short of achieving your goal, your mind is now hung up on the idea that you need to get back and finish the job. This tendency to obsess over interrupted or incomplete events is known as the "Zeigarnik Effect."

If you're a kayaker, there have probably been times when you've laid awake in bed thinking what a bad-ass boater you are now that you've conquered another gnarly river. You probably fell asleep to self-affirmations of paddling glory. The Zeigarnik Effect is the opposite of that feeling. It's that head spin you feel or "mental tension" that eats away at you until you've gone back and finished what you started. It's the nagging feeling in the back of your head that won't go away until you accomplish

Scott Springer in Hells by Travis Lehman

whatever it is that's left undone.

The human mind is strongly wired to reach closure. Kayakers know this feeling all too well. Every boater has probably said to themselves at some point, "I've got to get back there and finish that run." Off the river, we experience this need to get things done, too. "I need to finish my degree." "I need to apologize to so-and-so for all the fucked up shit I did when I was drunk." "One day, I'm going to finally beat Super Mario Bros. and free the princess from that jerk, Bowser."

These are the types of lingering thoughts that keep popping up while we're trying to move on with our lives. These annoying reminders about loose ends from our past stick with us so tightly that eventually, we resolve to get them done, or we continue to stuff them down and deal with the build-up of stress they cause. If we choose the former, we focus on the task, commit to following through, and ultimately, conquer whatever it is that we were working on, finally silencing the voices in our head. Completing these tasks relieves us of the tension and frees us to move on to the next challenge. The next river, the next degree, the next apology, the next video game. Completing goals, even the little ones, also helps build our self-esteem and produces feelings of achievement. It's gratifying to accomplish a goal, especially one that has been chewing on your brain for a long time. So while the Zeigarnik Effect might seem like a pain in the ass, it's a great motivator to get things done and feel great about what you've been able to accomplish.

FROM THE RIVER

Walking off a river is a blow to my ego. Going back
and walking off the same river again ten years later is
downright humiliating. But going back a third time eleven
years later and finally crushing the lines is one of the best
feelings I've had in a boat.

First Attempt at Hells Canyon — Spring 2007

It was cold and overcast the first time I attempted Hells
Canyon. Ben, Pat, and I made our way there, armed only
with the knowledge from my trusted guidebook Montana
Surf. We headed south of Big Timber, into a deep forested
canyon none of us had ever seen before. We'd heard that
the gauge was flowing somewhere around 3,500 cfs, but
we knew the gauge wasn't accurate since it was located
in Big Timber, about 40 miles downstream of Hells. With
multiple tributaries adding runoff between Hells Canyon
and Big Timber, we estimated that the flow would be a
manageable 1,200-1,700 cfs in Hells. Boy, were we wrong.

When we got to the footbridge marking the take-
out of Hells, we found the river at flood stage. Not ideal
conditions for a personal first descent. But the three of
us had paddled a lot of big water together that spring, we
trusted our abilities, and we trusted each other. The beta
in the book didn't sound too intimidating, citing "plenty
of eddies at all water levels" and one crux move about
halfway down. We decided to give it a shot and thought the
worst case would be that we do a lot of portaging. So the
three of us drove up the narrow dirt road to put in on the
swollen Boulder River to have a big water adventure.

The water level was so high that any eddy we tried to

catch was in tree branches and shrubs, no place you want to be snagged. Eventually, we found an eddy suitable for a quick scout. But the challenge with trying to scout a river flowing at this level is that it's genuinely one continuous rapid. There's no way to memorize lines or anticipate what's around the next bend. You're mainly just looking for lethal hazards to avoid — not a good situation for three paddlers descending an unfamiliar run at high flows.

We agreed that we would do our best to eddy hop down the right bank until we came to the next area to scout. That plan quickly went to shit. It didn't take long for the dominant force and speed of the river to separate us. The moment of truth came when I tried to make what felt like the world's widest ferry from my position on river left to Pat and Ben's location on river right. I blew the move and ended up getting surfed up against the right wall where the river makes a sharp dog-leg to the left. I held onto the rock wall to brace myself while looking down into a massive hole with a log wedged in its center. Trying to stabilize myself as my boat surged up and down from the violent pillow wedging me between the cliff and boiling whitewater, in a moment of panic I called for help. Pat was out of his boat and above me on the rock wall in a matter of seconds. I tossed my paddle onto the bank and clung on to the cliff to hold my boat in position and not wash into the hole. Once Pat got a hand on my life jacket, I pulled my skirt to climb up.

As we regrouped for the first time since our one-and-only scouting attempt miles upstream, we saw that the river didn't let up. With concerned looks on our faces, we contemplated our next moves. I admitted how rattled I was by the close call and worried about what else we might be downstream. Pat and Ben were gracious enough to concede the run as well. Despite not knowing how far it would be, or whether or not the crux was still waiting for us downstream, we decided to make one last ferry to river left and walk to the takeout. Our big water paddling adventure was over.

Five minutes into our hike, the footbridge appeared signaling the take-out. Without realizing it, we had paddled the entire stretch, only to walk the last few hundred yards. We all laughed when we saw the take-out, but I was devastated inside. Not only had I blown the ferry which got me pinned, but my lack of confidence cost us the run. Like all good paddling buddies should, Pat and Ben laughed it off and there were no hard feelings. But in my mind, I felt like it was my fault that we didn't complete the mission.

Second Attempt at Hells Canyon — Spring 2015

It was a sunny and hot day, and I was with a new crew on my second attempt. Eight years after my first failure to complete the run, I saw with my own eyes that the USGS Big Timber gauge read 2,700 cfs, which was less water than my earlier attempt. That felt like a manageable level to go back and finish what I had started nearly a decade earlier. Connor, Patrick, Scott, and I headed into the canyon to take a look and decide if we wanted to run it or not.

Given the run's hellish reputation, my story of carnage wasn't the only one those guys had heard. None of us were 100 percent determined to paddle Hells that day. We all agreed that, depending on the water level, the section below Hells called "Bible Stretch" would be a fun Plan B.

Once we got to the take-out, I noticed that the river looked higher than I expected from the gauge reading. But I was relieved that it wasn't at the same flood stage as it was the first time I ran Hells. We decided to drive up a bit and hike down to the river and try to see the rapids. We parked about two miles up the road and hiked down a giant scree field until we got a glimpse of the water. The river was raging. It wasn't as high as the first time, but it looked fast and mean. My survival instinct warned me to stay away. But my own personal Zeigarnik Effect told me to get my ass in my boat and do what I came there to do.

We deliberated for a bit until deciding to paddle it. I took comfort knowing that Patrick and Connor were both great paddlers. Patrick and I had kayaked a local creek a few days prior, and it wasn't until after the run that he told me he couldn't see anything because his contacts came out on the first rapid. Connor wore steel-toed boots instead of booties. I figured, if there's anyone you want to be on the water with when shit goes down, it's a guy in steel-toes.

Our experience was very different than my first trip down. The water was on the high side of good, there were nice eddies, and we found an established trail on river left for scouting. But the river was still powerful, requiring strong moves. At one point I was getting surfed in a hole when Connor shot over the upstream ledge and joined me, both of us now getting worked by the hydraulic. Eventually, we both swept out, still in our boats. Shortly after the party-hole with Connor, we paddled through the crux and toward the wall that had spooked me on the first trip. Cautiously, we decided to portage the dogleg. We stood on top of the cliff where eight years prior I had resolved to walk off the river. This time, I felt confident and ready for the last few hundred yards.

Patrick asked me if there was anything else downstream that we needed to worry about. I told him that it was more of the same Class IV boogie water and that I would lead the rest of the way. I might as well have said, "Hold my beer and watch this." Not 30 seconds after getting back in our boats, I was swept over a sticky hole and getting worked. I felt my boat going end over end as I fought to roll and gasp for air. I battled as hard as I could but ended up swimming.

Again, I was just a few hundred yards away from the take-out, and I had let my guard down. I was confident that I had the rest of the run in the bag, but the river had other ideas. Because of my complacency, I ended up losing my paddle and taking the walk of shame to the footbridge once again.

Third Attempt at Hells Canyon — Summer 2018

It was a warm and sunny day the third time I went back to Hells. Even though it had been eleven years since my first failed attempt and only two short years since my second, I felt like an entirely new person. I had taken the previous year off from kayaking to focus on sobriety and relationships. During that sabbatical from the river, my mind shifted. I was now two and a half years sober, and my head was in a new place. I no longer viewed kayaking as a means to prove something to myself or fill a void in my life. I now saw the river for what it was — water flowing down a stream bed, with an ebb and flow of the seasons. I didn't need to conquer Hells Canyon, I just needed to enjoy it. No one can defeat a river. Even the mightiest dams will one day erode, and the rivers will merely redirect their flow.

All I needed to enjoy my day in Hells Canyon was to just relax and tap into that natural flow. Although my history on the run was less than stellar, I was happy to be back.

The Big Timber gauge read 1,800 cfs, lower still than any of my earlier attempts, but I didn't trust it one bit. One of my buddies, Zach, knew that from the Hells Canyon campsite, we could bushwhack our way to an overlook that would give us a clear vantage point of the crux rapid. Even with my newfound perspective on kayaking, I couldn't help but feel a sense of fear and anticipation as we hiked toward the water. It wasn't surprising that my body reacted that way, given my previous two experiences. Our bodies have a way of trapping emotions, and reminders of past events can unexpectedly bring those emotions to the surface. As we stood on the cliff a hundred feet above the river, I felt a massive sense of relief. The river looked manageable. The exploding haystacks of my last two runs were now mostly crashing wave trains. The submerged rocks creating boat-eating holes were now boofable ramps. The crux that I had paddled blindly twice was a series of straightforward Class IV moves. I knew today was going to be the day I paddled, not walked, to the footbridge.

The sun shone directly overhead as we got in our kayaks below the portage. I felt its heat through my helmet. The river was calm and teeming with life. A recent hatch of hundreds of lacewing swarmed just inches above the surface. Trout jumped, eager for the flying snacks. A bald eagle, alarmed by our colorful boats, leapt from a pine tree and soared over our heads and downstream.

It's in these moments that the magic of the river is felt, not just seen. Unlike hikers along the bank, admiring the scenery from afar, we were within the scenery, part of the river. I felt the water roll down my paddle blade and onto my hands. I watched it soak into my skin. I was part of the river.

This connection to the river stayed with me the entire day. Every ferry, boof, eddy turn, surf, brace, and stroke felt effortless and in tune with the water. I have never paddle so well in my life, and I hope one day I'm able to paddle like that again. I was fully immersed in the flow, present with each ripple of water.

Once we made it through the crux, I knew that two personal milestones waited downstream. The first one would be to make it past the left dogleg that pinned me the first trip. Next would be the hole that stole my paddle on the second trip. I knew they were both downstream, but I didn't worry because I was sucked so deeply into the present tense that each paddle stroke put me on a higher plane.

I recognized the familiar rock wall on river right as we approached the dogleg that pinned me a decade earlier and that I had portaged two seasons before. This time, there was no slowing down, no timidness, and no hesitation. I ran sweep as our crew paddled the rapid with ease. I immediately eddied out behind the rock wall that had been my nemesis twice before. In the eddy, I tipped my boat over and while underwater let out a prideful scream of exhilaration. I rolled upright and with a huge smile peeled back into the current. The next few hundred yards were like paddling on clouds. I knew there was a monster hole waiting for me downstream somewhere, but it didn't matter because I felt like my kayak was floating high above the waves. I could see my group eddied out below a large horizon line. They were sitting below the hole that

I swam out of my last time down. One more boof and I could silence the demons that had been haunting me for eleven years. I felt the water load up on the back of my right paddle blade as I approached the lip of the hole which caused me to swim and lose my paddle the season before. Instinctively, I initiated the boof stroke by pulling with my right arm and lifting my knees toward my chest. My boat made a resounding SPLAT as it skipped off the backside of the foam pile. Oh how sweet it is!

As we enjoyed the last hundred yards of mellower rapids, I felt a sense of satisfaction that I never had before. Not just because I had completed a run that had haunted me for years, but because of how I did it. I'd taken the prior year off to focus on sobriety and my marriage. My newfound mindfulness and appreciation for the river had rewarded me with one of the best days on the water I'd ever experienced.

The water glistened as sunlight shone through the thick canopy of trees lining the bank. As we floated under the footbridge, I didn't want to get out of my boat. I wanted that feeling to last forever, my connection with the river to remain. Resting my paddle atop my kayak, I reached down to feel the water. As I lifted my hands, I saw the sunlight reflecting off my wet fingers. I stared at my hands until the last drops soaked into my skin, a final reminder of my connection to the river.

LIFE LESSON

No goals worth achieving come easily. Those which require commitment and humility provide the most satisfaction.

RIVER GUIDE

FOR PADDLERS in southwest Montana, Hells Canyon of the Boulder is a stretch of whitewater shrouded in mystery. It's tucked deep in the Absaroka Beartooth Wilderness, with an irregular paddling season and no accurate gauge. Ask any local kayaker who has attempted paddling Hells and you'll see his or her eyes widen before telling their thrilling story.

One such account comes from local kayaking ambassador Dave Schroeder who describes Hells Canyon as a "challenging Class IV-V section that at higher flows is a never-ending procession of exploding haystacks and vicious hydraulics." I'm not the only one who gets scared in there or gets hypnotized by its siren song. Dave admits that every time he paddles it he's gripped and wonders why he keeps going back.

When the river isn't a non-stop freight train or bone dry, it's one of the best stretches of whitewater in Montana. But catching it at a reasonable level is

Hells Canyon by Zach Dewell

difficult due to its irregular seasonal flow of snowmelt. The gauge for this run is 40 miles downstream of Hells, therefore inaccurate and unreliable for flows through the upper canyon. Multiple tributaries, each with their own snowmelt ebbs and flows, pour into the Boulder River between Hells Canyon and the gauge. If you do happen to catch it at a good flow, you'll be rewarded with a fantastic whitewater experience.

The only thing easy about this stretch is running shuttle. Once on the water, the first obstacle is a portage that acts as a sentinel to voyagers passing through. About a quarter-mile below the put-in, the river bends to the right and drops into a congested boulder-and log-filled horizon line. Portage on the left and hike about 300 yards. Once you're in the canyon, the action begins with a few short rapids that eventually all blend together. A trail on river left parallels most of the section above the crux. Once in the crux, the walls form a box canyon, and it's tough to scout and portage. The crux rapid is long and ends with a giant boulder in the middle of the river and a ledge drop that takes up the entire right channel.

Shortly after the box canyon, the action tapers off. But remain vigilant. Both of my mishaps happened in the last quarter-mile above the take-out. Once you reach the footbridge, take out or continue downstream and paddle the lower Bible Stretch.

Fun Fact: Hells Canyon and Bible Stretch are aptly named because of their proximity to many private camps catering to church groups and Bible campers. I guess that makes this river holy water after all.

State: Montana
River: Boulder
Section: Hells Canyon
Difficulty: IV-V
Gauge: USGS Boulder River near Big Timber (Note: This gauge is about 40 miles downstream of Hells Canyon and isn't an accurate read on the water volume in Hells Canyon.)
Flow: 1,000-3,000 cfs
Distance: 3.5 miles
Gradient: 115 ft/mi

Take-Out: The footbridge is located about 40 miles south of the little town of Big Timber, Montana. From Big Timber, take Hwy 298 south alongside the Boulder River. Hwy 298 eventually turns into Main Boulder Road. There is a small dirt turnout leading to a wide footbridge about 14 miles south of Natural Bridge Falls Picnic Area. This footbridge is also the put-in for the Bible Stretch. *45.374872, -110.207699*

Put-In: Four Mile trailhead and campsite are located about 3 miles upstream from the take-out. There is a mandatory portage just .3 miles downstream. Take out on river left and hike about 300 yards below the sieve pile. *45.34205, -110.2317*

CHAPTER 15

GOLD RUSH

Chili Bar to Lotus, South Fork
American River

"I was born by the river in a little tent
And like the river I've been running ever since
It's been a long time coming
But I know change is gonna come."

— **Sam Cooke**

Robert, Bob, and Joe Booth on the North Fork American

IT IS SAID that "No man is an island." We are all connected in ways we don't always realize or appreciate. This connection is a vital part of what makes humans the most dominant species on the planet. Through evolution, our ability to organize and cooperate has propelled us to be masters of our domain. This connection allowed us to build shelters, protect one another, and travel great distances over land and sea. Humankind went from being one of many competing species of primates into forming complex social structures that developed into communities, then cities, then countries. While there were undoubtedly influential leaders and remarkable individuals that helped shape the vision and motivate the masses, it was the collective power of the group that got us on top of Everest and landed us on the moon.

This dependence on the group is so innate to who we are as humans that when the connection is lost, often we are lost, too. In this modern era of social media, isolation and loneliness come with the Instagram territory.

Ironically, the immediate connections we make online through social media posts and YouTube videos can leave us feeling alone. In a congested digital world of influencers, friends, and followers we may feel more inadequate and disconnected than ever.

For those of us who love adventure, we often emphasize self-reliance. While being able to take care of yourself may seem like a positive attribute, it can lead to a false sense of security and emotional insensitivity. None of us adventurers are entirely self-reliant. We've all needed the help of others to get us where we are today. You probably didn't build your own kayak or sew your lifejacket — you bought those from someone. Which means you had to earn money by getting a job — a job that requires a skill that someone taught you in the first place.

In my experience of living out of my truck for three summers, those individuals who choose isolation are usually lonely and a little bonkers. A grown man that lives alone in the woods typically isn't a happy person. They didn't just run to the woods because they love the smell of pine trees, they ran away from something in their past. Paddlers like me who live out of vans searching for new rivers are often just as desperate for the camaraderie that comes with kayaking as we are for the adrenaline that fuels it. But when the trip is over, they're back in their van, and the adventure buddies are gone. It can be a sad, lonely existence, filled with adventure and excitement but devoid of any real connection. Without the likes they get on social media, there's no one around to affirm them as people.

There was a time when I was close to losing everything and living in a van down by the river. I wanted to escape the pain and responsibility of the real world. I wouldn't bother anybody, and no one would bother me. I didn't think I needed anybody in my life. I thought I was completely self-reliant and capable of handling any situation on my own. I was naive and arrogant. It wasn't long before I realized that my well being was beyond my control, and that I needed the help of others more than ever before. My self-centered attitude was the problem, not the solution. I couldn't have held onto my marriage without the love of my wife. I wouldn't have kept my job without an understanding boss. I wouldn't have been able to sober up without my support groups. I needed people in my life. Without them, today I'd be a lonely drunk.

An ongoing 80-year-old Harvard study confirms that those who embrace their community usually live longer and happier lives than the "van down by the river" types. The same outlook that propelled our primitive ancestors into the evolutionary pole-position also helps us live more fulfilled and connected lives. The people with whom we spend our time have a strong influence on who we become and how we feel about ourselves. These connections shape our minds and aging bodies. It's crucial to get over resentments, forgive, be vulnerable, and own your actions. Our family and closest friends are our community, not the likes on social media or good-time Charlies that come and go. It's our authentic relationships and connection to others that makes us strong and keeps us healthy.

FROM THE RIVER

Some of the best memories of my childhood were formed between the banks of the South Fork American River. Only three and five years old when we were baptized in the whitewater, my brother, Robert, and I loved everything about the river. It was under the shade of the Chili Bar Bridge, the put-in for the South Fork, where Robert and I sought shelter from the intense summer sun, practiced reading water, and skipped stones while the "adults" loaded the rafts. When the boats were ready, we'd jump in with my mom and dad to paddle our way downstream. In the eddy beneath the bridge, we learned how to maneuver our raft and became fascinated by the clay nests of the cliff swallows clinging to the bridge's substructure. When I die, a portion of my ashes will be scattered along the banks beneath the bridge in the hope that someday, I might be part of one of those clay nests, eventually disintegrating into the current and reuniting with my memories downstream.

Unlike many of the other fathers we grew up rafting with, my dad wasn't a lone oarsman navigating the rapids while my mom and us kids sat passively to enjoyed the ride. Instead, we made our way down the river, each with a paddle of our own. I guess there's something manly about rowing your family down whitewater while the wife and kids giggle and scream with each splash of water over the bow. But our raft was different. I have vivid memories of my mom digging into the water with each paddle stroke, sporting her blue-blocker sunglasses and an oversized pink visor. We all paddled through the rapids together. Although subtle, I believe the difference made me appreciate the river better and the group effort it takes to have a successful day on the water.

Passengers on an oar-raft sit and wait for the rapids to come to them, bracing for impact and enjoying the ride. The crew of an oar-rig put their fate in the hands of someone else and carry no responsibility for the outcome. They're merely riding the raft while the oarsman does all the work. Some people spend their entire lives living like this — letting others control their outcomes. Paddle rafting is a different experience. It's a powerful, synchronized dance down the river. Everyone has a paddle and must work as a team to execute the maneuvers. The captain chooses the line down the rapid and calls the strokes, and then everyone paddles in unison, executing the proper instructions. This teamwork builds a strong sense of camaraderie and accomplishment when you make it through a rapid safely. You don't get that bond and confidence when you're just sitting on someone else's raft while they do all the work.

Decades after my youthful family days on the river, I found myself back on the raft with a slightly different crew. Five years earlier, my mom had withered away, her mind and body taken by Alzheimer's. Her death affected my dad, brother, and me all differently. Her passing impacted our relationships with each other. The way we copped varied for each individual. Instead of leaning into my family for support, I isolated and fell deeper into my addiction. My mom was absent from our boat and I felt a void in my heart as deep as the river canyon. But as all rivers do, the water also carried life-giving energy that day. In my mom's place sat my six-year-old niece, Estelle, and my wife, Brit. With my dad at the helm, Robert and I took our positions in front. Life had come full circle. While my mom was no longer with us, I was now the one with a wife paddling beside me. Robert was no longer a little kid skipping stones. Instead, he was one of the "adults" with a child to look after on the river. My dad was beaming with pride as we made our way downstream. He had his family back together, and we paddled as a family through each of the rapids.

We had weathered the storm of my mom's passing and the aftermath that accompanied such a painful experience. Today we were all reunited. The river brought us back together, and we needed to work as a team to make it safely downstream. As we shoved off the rocky bank below the Chili Bar bridge, swallows darted in and out of their clay nests under the bridge. Estelle settled into her spot and tightened her grip around the strap holding the cooler in the raft, just as I once did as a small child.

"Forward please," my dad called as we paddled in unison across the eddy line and into the current. As he held the paddle's T-grip with his left hand and straightened the boat out, I saw the tattoo on his tricep that he got as a memorial for my mom.

"Little right," he commanded. We dipped our blades and spun the raft slightly downstream.

Robert observed our position relative to the first rapid, Chili Bar Hole, as we drifted in the current to make sure we weren't dropping in until Estelle was ready. I thought of all the good and bad times my brother and I had experienced together. Brit, obviously sensing my emotion, rubbed my shoulder affectionately as Bob lined up the raft for the drop. I felt a great sense of love and gratitude for her; she had paddled the hardest rapids of my life with me and helped get me back in the boat when I swam.

"Forward hard!" Bob asserted as we built momentum to punch the hole. As a family in unison, we dug our paddles in and punched Chili Bar Hole, whitewater once again splashing over the bow of our family boat.

Families are like rivers. There will be seasons when the water is calm and low, and those when it's chaotic and high. But the river bed itself will always be there to support the water that flows through its banks.

RIVER GUIDE

Booth family on Trouble Maker circa 1987

CALIFORNIA'S SOUTH FORK of the American River is one of the most culturally significant waterways in the United States. In 1848, gold was discovered there, triggering the Gold Rush. Between 1848 and 1855, a surge of more than 300,000 ambitious, gold-seeking adventurers from around the world flocked to the banks of the American River watershed. Included in these migrant workers was the infamous gold panner and whitewater pioneer, Zeek Gentile. Along with nuggets of gold, Zeek bagged countless first descents as he explored the streams of Gold Country. Although Zeek disappeared running what would later be known as Tunnel Chute on the Middle Fork American, to this day his legacy of whitewater exploration lives on.

A fun stretch for all ability levels, the South Fork is quintessential Class III. It offers numerous Class II-III+

rapids, with plenty of slack water, play-holes, and eddies in between. Chili Bar Hole greets paddlers at the put-in, ideally situated to surf a full-sized raft and collect the inevitable swimmers in gentle eddies. Shortly downstream comes the first real challenge — Meat Grinder, a quarter-mile long Class III with holes, lateral waves, and boulders. While a fun rapid for any experience level, it can be treacherous for a newbie or swimmer. When learning to kayak as a kid, my dad made me walk this rapid until I was able to catch small eddies and hit my combat roll consistently. Luckily, on river-right, a stone trail built by Chinese immigrants during the Gold Rush lets tentative paddlers scout or portage.

More Class II-III rapids and surf holes await downstream as you make your way deeper into the canyon. There are plenty of places to pull off for lunch, swimming, or to pick seasonal blackberries. About 5 miles into the run comes the last major rapid, Trouble Maker, a challenging Class III+ that requires hole punching and quick maneuvering as the river drops through slots and zig-zags through an S-shaped channel. The polished grey rocks that form the banks of Trouble Maker are ideal for hanging out to enjoy the scenery or be entertained by the occasional raft flipping. Scout or portage on river-left.

Below Trouble Maker the whitewater slows to a relaxing Class II pace for three scenic miles through Gold Country. You'll float past Sutter's Mill, the site that sparked the Gold Rush. There's also convenient beach access to Marshall Gold Discovery State Historic Park, a fun place to walk with the family and see the reconstructed era of the Gold Rush.

State: California
River: South Fork American
Section: Chili Bar to Lotus
Difficulty: III+
Gauge: AW SF AMERICAN CHILI BAR
Flow: 1,000-8,000 cfs
Distance: 3.5 miles
Gradient: 27 ft/mi

Take-Out: Henningsen Lotus Park is located about an hour east of Sacramento, California. From Hwy 50, take exit 37, Shingle Road, up and over the overpass in Shingle Springs. Once over the highway, take a quick right to stay on Shingle Rd. Follow Shingle Rd for 11 miles as it turns into Green Valley Rd and Lotus Rd. Henningsen Lotus Park will be on your left. This is a paid parking area, so bring some cash.

Put-In: Chili Bar is about 25 minutes away from the take-out, just north of Placerville, California. From Lotus, hang a left back onto Lotus Rd and then turn right onto Hwy 49. Stay on Hwy 49 for 8.2 miles and then hang a sharp left on Hwy 139 W. Take 139 down the hill to a bridge. Once you cross the river, turn left into Chili Bar. This is also a paid parking area, so make sure your buddy brings cash, too.

CHAPTER 16

DOWNSTREAM

"I have tasted a life wasted, I am never going back again."

— Eddie Veder

THE VIEW FROM THE RIVER offers a unique perspective.
I've always loved floating near the bank and appreciating
the layers of earth that lay beneath the forest floor. It's
like looking into a cross-section of the ground with x-ray
vision. On the surface, I can see where leaves and sticks
gradually disintegrate to become soil. Root systems from
various plants poke out where the soil and sand mix with
rocks. Tree trunks hang overhead with their knotted root
balls holding tightly to the large boulders at the waterline
where the ground meets the river. It's a very different view
when I hike through trails in the woods. While walking, all
I see is the top layer of sticks and leaves beneath my feet.
But from the river, I realize that much more lies beneath
the surface. It's a reminder that there are many more
layers to our lives, the people in them, and the challenges
we all face.

One of my favorite views of the river happens the
moment immediately after I've run a big rapid. From
here, I can glance back upstream and see the challenge I

Joe Booth by Pat Rogers

just overcame. Floating within the misty line where the water meets the wind, while feeling the surging water beneath my boat is the only place where I can experience this moment of reflection. Scouting and running a rapid are moments of deep concentration and flow. But when I make it safely to the bottom, I can let my guard down and enjoy the cascading water and steep rocky banks. They're much more beautiful after I've paddled down the rapid and look up at it for the first time with a racing heart and wet hands. It's a new perspective of the river, a new outlook on life. The rapid is the same one I had scouted from shore, but now I see it from the river — I see it through experienced eyes.

Scouting, committing, and successfully running a rapid offers experiences that can't be gained by reading books about paddling or watching YouTube videos. Looking back upstream and feeling the accompanying pride, both humbles and motivates me to continue downstream. Being armed with this type of real-life experience prepares me for the next challenge and puts me in a position to help others who may face this same challenge someday. It also makes me appreciate all the people who helped me get to where I am today. Without their help, I wouldn't have been able to get where I am today.

The exact same principles apply to recovery as they do the river.

When you're in the throes of addiction, it's impossible to have a clear view of the devastation you're causing yourself and those around you. But after a short period of sobriety, clarity forms. You begin to realize the impact your addiction has had on your life and the lives of others. Mixed emotions of joy and relief surface because you're finally putting your life back together, but shame and guilt arise for the pain you've caused.

Addiction feels like you're swimming down a Class V rapid. It's terrifying and disorienting. You can't breathe. The roar mutes all other sounds. Your body spins around, causing you to lose a sense of direction. You can't see anything but white light shining through tiny bubbles. Your fear instincts kick in, and thoughts of drowning enter your mind. You feel like there's nothing that you or anyone can do to help. You feel hopeless and alone as you wash downstream, gasping for air, and desperate for the shore.

This is what it feels like to be desperately trying to stop your destructive behavior — alone, unable to breathe, disoriented, senses dulled by the thunder of addiction.

This loneliness and isolation can lead to poor decisions and justification for bad behavior. "I'm only hurting myself" is a mantra for the addict living in denial. This self-centered thinking makes us insensitive and neglectful to those around us, which compounds the feeling of loneliness and stops us from realizing how our actions are affecting others.

When my wife confronted me about my behavior and how deeply I'd been hurting her, I realized that I wasn't the only one swimming down the river. My actions had pulled her into the rapids, too. My addiction didn't just affect me — it was also drowning Brit. Faced with a broken marriage and broken heart, Brit had every right to swim to shore and let me float downstream into oblivion. But she didn't. Brit did the hardest thing that any spouse to an addict could do — she stuck by my side and helped me get to shore, so I could breathe again. This heart-wrenching act of unconditional love was the most compelling event of my recovery. For the first time in as long as I could remember, I didn't feel alone. I felt accepted. I was open, raw, vulnerable, and yet Brit made me feel like my sobriety was worth fighting for because she was worth fighting for.

Like many alcoholics facing an ultimatum of getting a divorce or sobering up, I chose the latter. At first, I did it to save my marriage, but it didn't take long for me to realize that I needed to do it to save myself. Still, I knew I couldn't do it on my own. Finally, at rock bottom, I realized that I needed help from others. I needed help from experts. Like AJ, the sightless kayaker I paddled with on the Yellowstone River, I was trying to navigate recovery blind. I needed guides to show me the line. I needed to be with people who had experienced what I was going through and made it safely downstream. And like AJ, I needed to have the courage to face the darkness.

The best way to get good at something is to surround yourself with people who already have what you want. As my carnage stories attest, becoming a solid boater was no easy task. I couldn't have done it without the support of other paddlers. I surrounded myself with kayakers that I wanted to emulate — people who were bold, strong, graceful, loved nature and had different paddling styles. I learned as much as I could from them and applied it to my practice. Despite all the swims, tears, and self-doubt, eventually I found myself leading others down Class V rapids safely.

I now apply this lesson to my life off the water, too. I seek out mentors who exhibit the values and success that I want in my personal and professional life. I no longer think that I have to figure it all out on my own.

Now I appreciate that accepting help from others can enhance my skills and abilities. The depth of knowledge and guidance my mentors offer is humbling. By having a diverse set of role models to help me find my flow, I've learned that principles for success and happiness can be applied across disciplines. Like kayakers with different backgrounds, they have shown me creative ways to approach problems and overcome challenges. For example, a paddler with strong playboating skills has a fast roll and can get out of sticky holes. A paddler that focuses on creekboating has a strong boof and excellent eddy-hopping skills. Both of these paddling styles can be combined to make a well-rounded kayaker and open the river up to more opportunities.

Just as there are many lines down a river, for addicts seeking sobriety, there are many paths to recovery — inpatient rehab, outpatient rehab, religion, support groups, counseling, medication-assisted treatment, therapeutic recreation, adventure therapy, and an entirely new category of growing technologies like mobile health (mHealth), eLearning, and other online resources. To be successful in your recovery, you don't have to choose only one. Most people try different combinations until they find a program that works for them. There's no right or wrong way to get to the take-out of a river, but you do have to commit. You have to paddle out of the eddy at the top of the rapid and commit to making it downstream. How you make your way there is up to you.

Even with all the experts and tools to help, sobriety doesn't always mean happiness — but it's undoubtedly a step in the right direction. Here's the insidious thing about addiction — it's not the core problem; it's the solution to the problem. Wait. What? Addiction is a solution? Sorta. Take a step back and think about why people fall into substance or behavior abuse in the first place. Usually, they are unconsciously self-medicating. To cope with the pain of life, they seek a pleasurable or numbing escape, which eventually spirals into an unwanted harmful behavior that they can't stop — an addiction. The tragedy is, this kind of solution doesn't solve anything — instead, addiction makes matters worse.

Another way to think of addiction is as a symptom of a greater malady. You can't just treat the symptom and expect the problem to go away. You have to address the root cause of the symptom. While I can't promise that a person will win the happiness jackpot if they get sober, I can guarantee they won't get another DUI if they don't take another drink. And that's a good thing. But if a person wants to find long-term contentment, they need to deal with more than their sobriety — they must have the courage and commitment to look inward and face the source of their suffering.

For me, sobering up was just one step toward contentment and joy. I also needed to work through the underlying issues that caused the psychological pain I was trying to dull in the first place. For me, it was a lifelong struggle with self-esteem and anxiety. For as long as I can remember, I felt like an outsider — a scared, awkward kid from a poor family with yellow teeth and skinny shoulders. Although that's not how it appeared from the outside, it's how I felt on the inside. As a teen, the way I coped with these negative beliefs was by trying to prove that I was more popular, athletic, or attractive than my peers. This behavior led to unhealthy thoughts, actions, and habits.

As a young adult, I continued to struggle with those same issues. Eventually, some major life traumas occurred, which threw me into a downward spiral. Addiction offered temporary relief, but the pain of real-life was always waiting when I returned.

The humbling and uncomfortable process of becoming sober put me on a journey of self-discovery, which allowed me to work through the demons I had been fighting since I was a kid. It also showed me that I could finally accept myself, warts and all, while simultaneously working towards becoming the man I wanted to become. Removing addiction from my life was a step in the right direction, but it was only one step on the journey to recovery.

When we remove something from our life, it leaves a void that acts as a vacuum. Cutting out addiction allows us to channel that energy into something positive. The brain has a desire for equilibrium. So, it's essential to build new thoughts, beliefs, actions, and habits that result in our desired self. For me, that meant putting the *Class Five Mind* into action. Like most things in life, the more we practice something, the stronger those new neural pathways will form and reinforce the new habits. If not, we'll slide back into old behavior patterns and open the door for our past demons to haunt us once again.

Like deciding to portage a rapid on a river, sobriety is an act of humility and commitment. You accept that you've made the decision to stop using, and you move on with life — just like a kayaker with an injured shoulder takes time to recover from the injury. Eventually, your shoulder will be back to 100 percent. Smart paddlers won't put themselves in positions that could re-injure the joint the same way again. They'll work on proper paddle techniques to keep their shoulders in a safer and stronger position. There's no pity-party or whining about not being able to paddle like they used to. They learn proper form and become a better paddler because of it. These new skills take them further than the old ways, which held them back and led to their injury in the first place. Although it might have been painful and challenging, the damaged shoulder and its subsequent recovery helped them progress past their limitations. They learned ways of handling rough water.

This is what getting sober is all about — progression. As an addict, the old ways of coping with life's stress were holding me back in ways I didn't realize. Instead of confronting my problems and learning how to overcome them, I withdrew. My relationship with my wife was in shambles, my finances were a wreck, and my mental health was deteriorating. I tried to escape the reality I had built for myself, but running away didn't solve my problems, it only created more. It wasn't until I developed the *Class Five Mind* that I was able to apply the lessons from the river to my own life. Like the kayaker fighting a shoulder injury, I had to commit to healing and learning more advanced skills. I had to progress as a man. That's what recovery did for me. As the days, months, and years of sobriety float by, it becomes clear that the addictions I once relied on were holding me back the way a shoulder injury would for kayaking. Once I moved beyond that limitation and developed new habits — keeping my hands in a box, and my mind out of one — I was ready to take on more significant challenges in life.

While I no longer consider myself an alcoholic or addict, I say it with caution. The belief that someone can be "cured" of addiction is controversial and can be a slippery slope. While I'm not interested in debating the semantics or implications of identifying as "sober," a "recovered addict," versus an "addict," I genuinely believe that people can change. With a growth mindset, amazing things are possible. But I also feel that some things aren't worth testing.

No one has ever told me that their life got better once they started drinking again. So why risk it? The bars will always be grimy places with piss-covered urinals and loud stumbling people. You, on the other hand, will have evolved into a better version of yourself — someone you are proud of. Like a river valley after a long day of paddling, you can put addiction in your rearview mirror too.

Not all things in life are binary, but for those afflicted with addiction, sobriety should be. This humble act of surrender is the best way to guarantee long-term happiness. I once asked a guy with 25 years of sobriety how he did it. To which he replied, "I just stopped drinking." Binary. He then began to elaborate on the 12 Step work he did with other addicts to fill the gap that he had once tried to fill with booze. Through his work with other recovered addicts, he learned new coping skills, and engaged behaviors he wanted to cultivate within himself. It's also important to understand that his 25 years of sobriety happened one day at a time. Just like you can only paddle a river one stroke at a time. There's no use in worrying about the rapids downstream until you get to them.

In my experience, every addict I know who has experienced a relapse severely regrets the decision to experiment with drinking again. Sometimes it only takes one drink to plunge them into a bender. For others, it can be the gradual effect of letting addiction slowly take over and damage the years of progress they've made. The decision to drink again usually happens when they're careless or smug. A moment of complacency like this almost caused me to drown on the Madison River. That near-death experience taught me that when the consequences are high, it only takes one split second of letting your guard down or one wrong decision, and you can find yourself fighting for your life.

What if relapse does occur? Start over. Just because you flipped over and ended up swimming doesn't mean your day on the water is over. Swim to shore, empty the water from your boat, and catch your breath. Then think about what caused you to swim, and adjust, so it's less likely to happen again. Yes, a relapse is a setback, but it doesn't mean that you can't try again. I swam three times on Tobin, the first Class V run I ever attempted. But I kept getting back in my boat and eventually made it to the take-out. Fifteen years after that demoralizing event, I went back to Tobin and led a friend down the run safely. This is when resilience and commitment come into play. If you relapse, it's not the end of the world. You have a chance to redeem yourself, and you can also use what you've learned to help someone else on their journey.

For me, river running is a cycle that requires all the principles of a *Class Five Mind*: humility, courage, commitment, resilience and flow. When I scout a difficult rapid, I must be humble when looking for lines of safe passage. Once I've determined a route that I'm comfortable with, I must summon the courage to walk back to my boat and take action. As soon as I cross the eddy-line into the current, I'm committed to the run. If something goes wrong and I flip, I must be resilient by rolling back up and continuing downstream. All these moments put me in the flow, resulting in a successful run and a new perspective on the river. As I float downstream toward the next horizon line, the cycle repeats itself. This is what life is like — moving along and continuously facing new horizons, challenges, and opportunities. We can't control the waves that rock our boat, but we can determine how we react to them.

As Victor Frankl wrote in his book *Man's Search For Meaning*, "Our answer must consist, not in talk and meditation, but in right action and in right conduct." The *Class Five Mind* is made up of the five principles that I identify with most. It's a recipe that works for me, but you can choose your own line if you don't identify with them. What's important is you select words you can put *action* behind.

This is my story from the river to sobriety. Now I just ask two things — Whatever you're striving for 1). Don't give up on yourself; and 2). Help others along the way.

There's a take-out waiting for you downstream. Keep paddling.

ABOUT THE AUTHOR

JOE BOOTH is a lifelong whitewater enthusiast and outdoorsman. He has worked as a kayaking instructor, river guide, safety boater, and volunteer for numerous paddlesports organizations across the Western states. Through his own journey of finding a balanced life free from addiction, Joe has gained insight into the many challenges people face on and off the water. He is active in the outdoor behavioral health industry, using outdoor experiences as a path to healing.

Joe has spent the past 20 years studying the fields of motivation, adult learning, peak performance, and behavioral psychology. He combined the knowledge from these subjects to personally reconstruct himself from being a self-proclaimed "dirt-bag" living out of his truck, into a top performer with billion-dollar software companies in Silicon Valley. Joe is recognized as a thought leader in the field of corporate development, speaking at conferences, and training high-performance operations and sales teams.

Joe is the founder of Class Five Mind, a leading recovery platform that combines technology with science-based techniques for overcoming addiction. He also sits on the Board of Directors for Voyager, a non-profit dedicated to helping people heal through outdoor experiences.

ACKNOWLEDGEMENTS

THIS BOOK wouldn't have been possible without the continued support of numerous people from many different walks of my life.

To my beautiful and amazing wife, Brit Booth, for all of the support and encouragement, for tolerating my years of excitement about this book, and for being an inspiring role model of courage, commitment, humility, resilience, and flow. To my fantastic editor and mentor, Eugene Buchanan, for guiding me through the book writing process and helping me navigate the rough waters. To my talented design team of Ben McKenzie, Josh Endres, Rob Peters, and David Carroll for adding style to these pages and making my words come to life. Matt Larson, Paul Kuthe, and Nick Hinds for their support and suggestions during the early development of this book.

My late mother, Maria Booth, for introducing our family to the South Fork American River. My dad, Bob Booth, for teaching me how to paddle. My brother, Robert Booth, for showing me my first lines. To my loving and gracious in-laws, the Obstars, for welcoming and accepting me. Al Eggleston and the rest of the River Sharks for making paddling fun as a kid.

Marya C. Endriga Ph.D. for introducing me to psychology and continued mentorship. Chip Kern MS LCPC and Andy Lear LCSW for their patience and guidance.

Participants and staff at First Descents, Team River Runner (especially AJ), and Eaglemount, for all of the inspiration of courage and resilience. American Whitewater for protecting the access and water of our nation's streams. To the strong men and women at the

Bozeman Fellowship Hall.

Special thanks to the photographers and paddlers who generously contributed their photos in support this book: Bob, Maria, and Robert Booth, Zach Dewell, Kevin Kennedy, Dave Schroeder, Joe Vincent, Connor Fitzgerald, Gregory Lee, Mareike Delley, Victor Bézard, Cyrille Delley, Dave Steindorf, Wes Schrecongost, Todd Wells, William and Sam Freihofer, Ford Smith, Travis Lehman, Scott Springer, Andrew Daigh, Nick Gottlieb, Matt Mounsey, Forest Ledger, Neil Seifert, Pat Rogers, Kenya Otto, John and Diana Ferpo, Aurelia Bergamo.

Special thanks to Joe Mornini at Team River Runner and Brad Ludden at First Descents for inspiring me to think beyond my own boat and aspire to paddle for a purpose.

To all of the paddlers I've shared the water with over the years, thanks for helping me get to shore, empty my boat, make the portage, drive the shuttle, probe the line, set safety, pump me up, calm me down, and prove that kayaking is a great team sport.